THE WO

ALEXIS
SANCHEZ

Also by Tom and Matt Oldfield:

Luis Suárez: El Pistolero

Eden Hazard: The Boy in Blue

Gareth Bale: The Boy Who Became a Galáctico

Wayne Rooney: Captain of England

Raheem Sterling: Young Lion

THE WONDER BOY
ALEXIS SANCHEZ

TOM AND MATT OLDFIELD

DINO

Published by Dino Books
an imprint of John Blake Publishing Ltd
3 Bramber Court, 2 Bramber Road,
London W14 9PB, England

www.johnblakebooks.com

www.facebook.com/johnblakebooks ▪
twitter.com/jblakebooks ▪

First published in paperback in 2016

ISBN: 978 1 78 606 013 6

British Library Cataloguing-in-Publication Data:

A catalogue record for this book is available from the British Library.

Design by www.envydesign.co.uk
Cover illustration by Dan Leydon
Background image: Shutterstock

Printed in Great Britain by CPI Group (UK) Ltd

5 7 9 10 8 6 4

Papers used by John Blake Publishing are natural, recyclable products made from
wood grown in sustainable forests. The manufacturing processes conform to the
environmental regulations of the country of origin.

Every attempt has been made to contact the relevant copyright-holders, but some
were unobtainable. We would be grateful if the appropriate people could contact us.

For Noah and the future Oldfields to come

Looking forward to reading this book together

TABLE OF CONTENTS

CHAPTER 1 – **WINNING AT WEMBLEY** 11

CHAPTER 2 – **TOCOPILLA** 16

CHAPTER 3 – **THE HERO OF CANCHA LAZARETO** 21

CHAPTER 4 – **FOOTBALL BOOTS I** 26

CHAPTER 5 – **SCHOOL DAYS FOR 'DILLA'** 31

CHAPTER 6 – **FOOTBALL BOOTS II** 37

CHAPTER 7 – **THE NUMBER 10 ROLE** 43

CHAPTER 8 – **SCOUTED** 49

CHAPTER 9 – **EARLY DAYS AT COBRELOA** 55

CHAPTER 10 – **PLAYING WITH THE BIG BOYS** 62

CHAPTER 11 – **NEXT STEPS TO GREATNESS** 68

CHAPTER 12 – **INTEREST FROM ITALY** 75

CHAPTER 13 – **CHAMPION OF CHILE** 83

CHAPTER 14 – **AN ARGENTINIAN EDUCATION** 90

CHAPTER 15 – **READY FOR SERIE A** 97

CHAPTER 16 – **ALEXIS & ANTONIO** 104

CHAPTER 17 – **BEGINNING AT BARÇA** 111

CHAPTER 18 – **THE WONDER BOY IS BACK** 119

CHAPTER 19 – **THE RIGHT PLACE AT THE RIGHT TIME** 126

CHAPTER 20 – **HEARTBREAK IN BRAZIL** 134

CHAPTER 21 – **GUNNING FOR GLORY** 141

CHAPTER 22 – **PREMIER LEAGUE LIFE** 147

CHAPTER 23 – **TROPHY TIME** 152

ACKNOWLEDGEMENTS

This was a very special opportunity for us, as brothers, to work together on something we are both so passionate about. Football has always been a big part of our lives. We hope this book will inspire others to start – or continue – playing football and chasing their dreams.

Writing a book like this was one of our dreams, and we are extremely thankful to John Blake Publishing and James Hodgkinson and Chris Mitchell, in particular, for making this project possible. It was great to have your guidance and support throughout our writing process.

We are also grateful to all the friends and family that encouraged us along the way. Your interest and sense of humour helped to keep us on track. Will, Doug, Mills, John, James Pang-Oldfield and the rest of our King Edward VI friends, our aunts, uncles, cousins, the Nottingham and Montreal families and so many others – thank you all.

Melissa, we could not have done this without your understanding and support. Thank you for being as excited about this collaboration as we were. Iona, thank you for your kindness and encouragement during long, work-filled weekends.

Noah, we're doing our best to make football your favourite sport! We look forward to reading this book with you in the years ahead.

Mum and Dad, the biggest 'thank you' is reserved for you. You introduced us to football and then devoted hours and hours to taking us to games. You bought the tickets, the kits, the boots. We love football because you encouraged us to. Thank you for all the love, all the laughs and for always believing in us. This book is for you.

CHAPTER 1

WINNING AT WEMBLEY

'*Alexis Sánchez baby, Alexis Sánchez oooohhhhhhhh!*'

Alexis could hear the Arsenal fans loud and clear as he warmed up on the Wembley pitch. He loved the song that they had made for him. There was still half an hour until kick-off but the atmosphere was already amazing. It was Arsenal's second FA Cup Final in a row but for Alexis, this was the chance to win a first English trophy, and what a trophy it was. Even as a kid growing up in Chile, Alexis knew about the oldest football competition in the world. It was a dream come true.

'Alexis, this is it,' Arsène Wenger said to him in

the dressing room before the game, but he knew he didn't really need to inspire his superstar. 'You've had an amazing first year here but you need to end it with a winner's medal!'

As Alexis walked out on to the pitch, holding the hand of a mascot, fireworks went off all over the pitch. The FA Cup trophy was sitting there, shining brightly and waiting for him. He couldn't wait to get the ball and run at the Aston Villa defence. He knew it would be a tough game but there was no way he was going to lose this match. Alexis had been the Arsenal hero in the semi-final, scoring both goals to beat Reading. And he was determined to be the hero again in the final.

'We need to stay focused and we need to be patient,' Alexis said to Mesut Özil and Theo Walcott, his partners in attack. 'If we play well, we will score in the end.'

Alexis was right. Aston Villa stopped them again and again but the Gunners didn't give up or get frustrated. At the end of the first half, the Gunners finally scored and it was thanks to Alexis. Nacho

Monreal crossed from the left and Alexis was there at the back post. He couldn't get enough power to head for goal so instead he headed the ball across to Theo, who smashed it into the back of the net. They had that goal they needed.

'I'm not done yet,' Alexis told Mesut once Arsène had given his half-time team talk. The important message was that they were only halfway to victory. 'I want to win but I also want to score!'

Five minutes into the second half, Alexis chased across the pitch to get to the ball first. The Aston Villa defenders backed away in fear of what he might do with his brilliant skill. Alexis had the space he needed for one of his trademark long-range shots. With his right foot, he hit the ball with so much power and swerve that the goalkeeper could do nothing as it sailed over his head. Alexis couldn't believe it; he had scored and it was one of his best goals ever.

Per Mertesacker scored a third and Olivier Giroud made it four. 4–0 – what a way to win the FA Cup Final! On the touchline, Arsène clapped and allowed himself to smile. He was very proud of his squad and especially his Chilean superstar. What a signing he had been.

'*Arsenal! Arsenal! Arsenal!*' Alexis shouted with his teammates at the final whistle. They were a close group of friends and they were in the mood for a party.

With an Arsenal scarf around his neck and a Chilean flag in his hands, Alexis was one of the first players to walk up the stadium steps to collect his medal from Prince William. As he passed, the fans high-fived him and patted him on the back. He was part of the Arsenal family now and he loved it. It was great to get the medal but what he really wanted was the trophy. Captains Per and Mikel Arteta were the first to lift it and then it was his turn.

Alexis shouted for joy as he raised it above his head. He kissed it twice and passed it on to Jack Wilshere.

'We did it!' Jack told him, giving him a big hug. He was wearing a silly red-and-white jester hat and he was having the time of his life.

It wasn't Alexis's first trophy but it was certainly one of his favourites. Down on the pitch, there were more fireworks and Theo sprayed champagne everywhere. The players thanked the fans by having photos taken with them. It was a really great celebration. Alexis wished that his family and friends could have come from Chile to share his special day but they had all sent him good luck messages.

It was an incredible way to end the best season of his career so far. Twenty-five goals and twelve assists was a new record for Alexis. The big-money transfer from Barcelona had put a lot of pressure on him to perform. He had worked really hard and the players and fans had made him feel so welcome. Arsenal Football Club felt like home and he was already excited about challenging for more trophies next year.

'Let's win the Premier League *and* the Champions League!' Alexis told Mesut as they posed for more photos.

He had come a long way from Tocopilla.

CHAPTER 2

TOCOPILLA

'Humberto! Alexis! Dinner is ready!'

Martina stood in the doorway of her house
calling for her young sons. They spent most of the
summer days playing out in the streets but food
usually brought them home. She used to make
them stay near the house but after a few broken
windows, she allowed them to play a little further
away. Tocopilla was a small town in northern Chile
and Martina knew many people she could call if
she was worried about them. The rule was that
Humberto had to take Alexis with him and keep
him safe. Alexis looked up to his older brother and
wanted to copy everything he did, and because

Alexis was already a good footballer, Humberto didn't mind him tagging along.

Martina's daughter Marjorie was already at home setting the table – she was the good child who always helped her mother, unlike her wild brothers. After she had called for the third time, Martina finally heard the familiar sound of running feet and saw her sons making their way down Tocopilla's long street, *Calle Orella*. Looking around her, Martina thought back to better days, when mining had brought money to the town. Now, however, there were rusted cars and crumbling buildings everywhere. The Sánchez home, made of clay and wood, was in real danger of falling down but there was nowhere else for them to go. The skies were grey with pollution and the people of Tocopilla were struggling. There was a reason why they called their town 'Devil's Corner'.

As they ran, Humberto and Alexis passed an old football between themselves. Each kick produced a big cloud of dust. In the distance, big waves broke on the seashore. Alexis was much smaller than

Humberto but he was always determined to keep up with his older brother. Martina could see the smiles on their faces from a hundred metres away.

'Sorry we're late, Mum,' Humberto said as they rushed through the broken metal gate. They were both out of breath and covered in sweat. 'It was a really important football match but don't worry, Alexis scored the winning goal!'

Alexis nodded with pride. 'It was a beauty, Mum, you should have seen it! We were playing against nine-year-olds and I dribbled past five of them. They tried to foul me but I kept going. I was just too quick for them!'

Martina wanted to be angry but looking at the grin on Alexis's face, that just wasn't possible. 'That's great, darling. Leave that filthy football outside please. Now go and wash yourselves quickly. Hurry, dinner's getting cold.'

The Sánchez family sat down together to eat lentils and rice. Without the support of her husband, Martina had to work very hard to feed her children and make sure that they had clothes to wear. She was a cleaner at the local school and in the summer when the term was over, she travelled over fifty miles a day to sell fish. Life was never easy. Uncle Jose did as much as he could to be a father-figure for the boys but he had a family of his own to look after. Looking at her sons as they wolfed down their food, she could see a few new holes in their clothes that she would need to sew up. And they would soon grow out of those garments and need more. Everything cost money. 'At least they are happy,' Martina thought to herself. She was desperate to protect her sons from the dangers that surrounded them, especially crime and alcohol.

In between mouthfuls, the room was filled with the sound of squabbling and laughter. Marjorie rolled her eyes as Alexis told the story of his winning goal for the tenth time. Each time, he added a new detail until it was the greatest goal ever scored.

'...and then I took it round another opponent, and then another and finally I flicked it up over my head and volleyed it into the top corner.'

His family soon brought him back down to earth.

'The way you tell it, there must have been fifty players on the team!'

'Top corner?! The goal didn't even have a net!'

'Son, you tell a great story but I don't believe a word you say!'

Alexis just shrugged his shoulders and smiled. He knew how good the goal was and that was all that mattered. He would dream about it for weeks, or at least until he scored a better one.

The boys had seconds and then thirds, and then washed and dried the dishes. Just as they sat down in front of the old TV to fight over the remote, Martina called out from the kitchen. 'Humberto, Alexis, come here! I have some jobs for the men of the house.'

Her sons groaned loudly. 'Mum, we're too tired – we've been playing football all day!'

'That's no excuse – we need wood for the stove, and there's a door handle that needs fixing. If you play all day, you have to work all night!'

CHAPTER 3

THE HERO OF CANCHA LAZARETO

Alexis put one rock down and then marked out five paces and put the second rock down. 'Is that big enough for the goal?'

'Yes, looks good – let's get this game started!' Sergio shouted from the other end of the pitch. This was *Cancha Lazareto*, their stadium, where the kids of Tocopilla played all day every day if they could. It wasn't perfect – there were no goals and only random patches of dry grass amongst the dirt – but it was good enough for now. Most of them played barefoot and so they spent a few minutes every morning clearing stones and rubbish into a pile in the corner. The only spectators were a pack of wild dogs that circled the town looking for scraps of food. They weren't scary but if they got too close to the pitch, the kids threw stones at them to keep them away.

'Why can't people just use bins?' Humberto asked as he collected up all of the beer cans.

They had fourteen players so far, enough for seven-a-side. Kids would come and go throughout the day but fourteen was a good start. Humberto and Juan were usually the team captains and they turned around while the others chose numbers.

'9,' Humberto called first and Diego, one of the weaker players, walked over to join Team A. Humberto did not look happy.

'3,' Juan called next and Gonzalo, one of the best players, joined Team B. 'Yes!' Juan cheered and high-fived his new teammate.

Humberto picked '2' and got Carlos, who could barely kick the ball; Juan picked '12' and got Dani, the best player in Tocopilla. The teams didn't look fair at all. Alexis was '11', the same number as his hero Marcelo Salas wore on his shirt for the

Chilean national side. Alexis was pleased to be on the same side as his brother but Humberto didn't see it that way.

'Their team is amazing,' he moaned, kicking at the dirt. 'We've got no chance.'

'Let's wait and see,' Alexis said with quiet confidence. He was ready for this. 'The Sánchez brothers can beat anyone!'

Alexis was the youngest and smallest player there but that didn't scare him. This was his favourite kind of football. He was used to playing against older kids, and he preferred it that way. He enjoyed the challenge, the test of his strength and skill. If opponents kicked him, it just made him more determined to beat them.

And Alexis was feeling good about today and he really hoped that Uncle Jose would turn up to watch the game. Jose often came down to Cuarta Poniente once he had finished his work for the day to cheer his nephews on. He seemed certain that Alexis would grow up to be a superstar – 'One day, I'll watch you on TV!' he often said when he came round for dinner. Jose was Alexis's biggest fan and he loved him for that.

The game kicked off and their team was soon 1–0 down. Carlos was in goal and he let the ball trickle slowly between his legs. Humberto was furious. 'What was that? You're rubbish!' he shouted, waving his arms around like a madman. Alexis put a hand on his brother's shoulder to calm him down. The game had only just begun; there was plenty of time left to win the match.

Humberto got the ball in the middle of the pitch. He looked to his left, and then to his right; none of his teammates were in space on the wings. What could he do? The only option was Alexis, who was playing the 'Salas' role as the striker. He looked tiny next to the big defender. Humberto played the ball into his brother's feet and watched in awe as he flicked it cleverly around his marker, dribbled past another and then fired the ball off the left rock and into the goal. 'Wow,' he said to himself. He didn't like it but he knew his brother would soon be much better than him.

Alexis celebrated with a somersault, landing perfectly on his feet. He had scored another great goal, and he imagined thousands of fans watching it on TV, cheering for him. He could feel his heart beating really fast in his chest; this was his favourite feeling in the world. He just wanted to do it again and again. So that's what he did. The pitch was quite small but they still couldn't keep up with him. And because he was so strong, they couldn't push him off the ball either. And when they managed to surround him, Alexis just passed it for Humberto to score instead. The Sánchez brothers were everywhere, making sure that Juan, Dani and Gonzalo didn't get a second of peace.

After an hour, their opponents called for a time-out. 'When did your brother become so good?' Juan asked as he lay in the dirt trying to get his breath back.

Humberto just shrugged. When *had* Alexis become so good? And just how good could he become?

CHAPTER 4

FOOTBALL BOOTS I

'Alexis, do a somersault for us!' Darío, their
neighbour called out, as he put a bowl of water
out for their dog, Perdita. The Sánchez brothers
were playing outside their house, throwing stones
at a paint can they had placed in the street. With no
breeze coming in from the sea, it was too hot
for football.

Alexis groaned – not again! He was tired of doing
his tricks. He wasn't a circus act.

'Come on, please! Look, here's a peso for you,'
Darío said, flicking a coin over the low fence to him.
Alexis's eyes lit up – another bit of money to put
towards his football boots. For that, he was happy to

entertain anyone. He'd been saving up for months and months, but he still had a long way to go.

Darío's young daughters came out to watch the big performance. If Alexis did the first one well, perhaps they would pay him to do another, and then another. He could only hope. He put all of his effort into making it the best somersault he'd ever done. He jumped as high as he could, tucked his legs tightly into his chest and bent his knees as he landed. Everyone clapped and he took a bow.

'Again! Again!' Darío's daughters cheered.

Alexis gave them a cheeky grin. 'Sorry, that'll be another peso!'

'An entertainer *and* a businessman!' Darío replied, reaching into his pocket for another coin.

Alexis smiled and got ready to do it all over again. He wanted football boots more than anything in the world. Most nights he dreamed about the day when he would put them on and lace them up. With proper boots, he would have so much more power for his shooting. He would be unstoppable.

Once their neighbours had enjoyed the

performance and gone back inside, Humberto tried to grab the money from his brother's pocket.

'Hey, get off me! What are you doing?' Alexis shouted, pushing him away.

'You know the rule – any money we make, we give to Mum. She needs us to help her.'

Alexis felt a little guilty but he was determined to make his dreams come true. 'That's only the money we get from washing and looking after cars. This is *my* money for football boots. And besides, buying football boots will help Mum more in the long run. I'm going to become a professional footballer and when I do, she'll never have to work again!'

Humberto rolled his eyes and walked back into the house. All of his friends had the same big dream. Alexis was much better than them but even so; growing up in a small port town, miles away from Santiago, the capital city, it was pretty unlikely that anyone would spot Alexis's talent. But he really hoped his brother was right to have such faith in his skills.

★ ★ ★

Every year at Christmas, the council drove a pick-up truck through the streets of Tocopilla giving out gifts to the people. It was a local tradition and the biggest day of the year for the young ones. For some of them, these might be the only presents they would get. Times were very hard for the people of Tocopilla.

'Kids, hurry, the truck will be coming soon!' Martina called out. Marjorie and Humberto were too old to get really excited about it, but Alexis still loved the event. He sprinted through the house and was the first one out on to the street. He loved the party atmosphere of the day, with loud music playing and the amazing smells of traditional Chilean cooking drifting through the air. Alexis had already had dinner but he suddenly felt very hungry. The adults laughed and danced, and the kids ran up and down the road, impatient for the arrival of the truck.

'Imagine if we get a new football,' Alexis said to his school friend Gustavo. 'Or maybe even football boots!'

'Don't be silly – they only ever give out sweets,'

Gustavo replied. He'd seen the truck too many times to get his hopes up anymore.

Alexis knew that was true but it didn't stop him from dreaming. If he wanted to be the best, he had to dream big. He had to believe that amazing things could happen to people who deserved it. So every year, he said his prayers and waited.

Finally, they saw the lights of the truck in the distance. The kids ran towards it, waving their arms and shouting out. In the back of the truck, there were lots of people holding bags and bags of sweets. As the truck drove along slowly, they threw them out to the waiting children. Kids battled with each other to collect the most bags. There were no footballs but Alexis was used to the disappointment. And besides, he liked sweets too.

'When I become a famous footballer, I'm going to drive the truck,' Alexis told Gustavo with his mouth full of chocolate. For once, he looked very serious. 'And it won't be sweets that I throw – it'll be signed footballs!'

CHAPTER 5

SCHOOL DAYS FOR 'DILLA'

'Today, we'll be talking about our childhood heroes,' the teacher said, walking around the classroom. She was pleased with what she saw. 'You've all brought in your pictures. Well done! They look lovely in the frames you've made. We'll take it in turns to talk about who we've chosen and why.'

Alexis looked around at his classmates. Some had spent a lot of time making their picture frames look really pretty with flowers and colourful patterns. Alexis didn't like art and so he'd got his sister Marjorie to help him. He liked his frame, though; it had footballs drawn along all four edges. He found it hard to sit patiently at a table and work carefully with his hands – he'd much rather be outside playing football with his feet.

A few of his classmates had picked members of their families; others had picked cartoon characters like Winnie the Pooh and Mickey Mouse. Now Alexis was worried that he had made the wrong choice. At first, he wanted to talk about Marcelo Salas, the Chilean striker who played in Italy. He scored lots of goals and was a national legend. However, he couldn't find a picture of him at home and so he had to think again.

'Alexis, it's your turn now,' the teacher said after a little while. 'Who have you chosen?'

He froze. He was pretty embarrassed now. 'Err, I picked … myself.'

Everyone laughed; they were used to Alexis's self-confidence. His mum had found a picture of him in an old shirt that Humberto had grown out of. He had a football at his feet and a winner's medal around his neck.

The teacher was too surprised to speak at first. 'Okay … why have you picked yourself, Alexis?'

His face went bright red; he didn't know what to say. Eventually, he replied, 'I'm a very good footballer and I can do lots of really cool skills. I'm fast, I'm strong and I work hard to make tackles. When I grow up, I'm going to be a famous footballer and win lots of trophies.'

This time, no-one laughed. Anyone who had seen Alexis play football knew that he was very talented and really determined to be the best. He believed he would be a superstar and so they believed it too. 'I'll buy you a car,' he would say with an arm around one friend's shoulder, 'and I'll buy you a house,' he would say to the friend on his other side.

Alexis didn't really like school and he never stayed a second longer than he had to. But with his mum as a school cleaner, he knew that she would find out straight away if he was naughty. Martina could be very scary when she got angry. Alexis found it hard to concentrate in class; he wasn't a bad student but it just wasn't where he wanted to be. He spent most of his days staring out of the window, waiting for break time so that he could go out and play football.

On the school playground, he was the star player. Very few could touch him, let alone tackle him. As he dribbled through player after player, it looked like he was dancing. He made it look so easy. The teachers would often come out to watch him play. Alexis always liked to have an audience.

'Not again! *Dilla*, you'll have to climb up and get that,' Gustavo complained as Alexis kicked the ball into a tree for the fifth time that week. He could strike the ball very hard – often too hard. Shooting was something Alexis knew he needed to practise more. It wasn't all about power; there was a target and he needed to stay calm and carefully aim at it every time.

'*Dilla*' was short for '*Ardilla*', the Spanish word for 'Squirrel'. The nickname had stuck for two reasons: firstly because of his speed in the playground but also because every time he kicked it too high, Alexis would rush up and get it back down. No-one could climb trees or roofs as quickly as *Dilla*. 'Sorry!' he shouted and he was up in the branches in seconds. They watched in fear as he climbed higher and higher but he had the perfect balance of a gymnast. In no time at all, the ball was back on the pitch.

His schoolmates knew they were watching someone special. '*Dilla* doesn't even know what fear is!'

The playground wasn't the only place where Alexis could impress. As a six-year-old he joined the local team, Club Arauco de Tocopilla, where he quickly became their star playmaker. He liked travelling to other cities in the region to play football but he wasn't very keen on their idea of training – lots of boring passing, tackling and shooting exercises. He just wanted to play proper matches.

'Oh, glad that you could join us. You're half an hour late – again!' shouted Alberto, the team coach, as he spotted Alexis sprinting out onto the field. 'What's your excuse this time?'

Alexis decided it wasn't worth lying. 'Sorry, Coach, I was playing football at Cuarta Poniente. The game went to penalties!'

Alberto rolled his eyes and shrugged. What could he do? Alexis was so much better and faster than the other players; there was no way he could drop him. The rest of the team weren't very happy either that Alexis often played street football rather than training with them, but he made up for it with his awesome skills. In one game, he won the ball in his own penalty area and dribbled past player after player after player. On the sidelines, Alberto couldn't believe what he was seeing. It must be magic. Alexis had just the goalkeeper to beat but on this really hot day, he was exhausted by the time he arrived in the penalty area. Just as he went to shoot, the goalkeeper fouled him.

Alexis could feel the pain in his leg and he was out of breath, but he got straight to his feet. 'I'm taking the penalty!' he shouted – and no-one argued with him.

CHAPTER 6

FOOTBALL BOOTS II

'Mum, I've been saving up for ages now, and I still don't have anywhere near enough money to buy football boots!'

Alexis hated to ask his mum for things but this was important. He was Arauco's best player and he had even travelled over a thousand miles to go to a training camp in Rancagua for one of the best teams in Chile, Universidad Católica. It was embarrassing to turn up wearing boots that weren't the right size because they were borrowed from someone at school.

Martina sighed loudly; she hated to disappoint her son. 'Alexis, I know how much this means to you, but we just can't afford it!'

Alexis stared down at the floor. 'Every time I play, I get blisters because the boots are too small. They don't need to be the most expensive boots, Mum; they just need to be *my* boots.'

'I know, darling, I know. Give me a month and let's see what I can do.'

Alexis nodded, but without money, he didn't see what his mum could do about it. Martina asked everyone she knew if they had any cheap football boots that she could buy, but not even the worst were cheap enough for her budget. In the end, she just gave up asking; she had seen her son play enough times to know that he needed the very best – not a pair of old, broken boots.

Martina's last resort was to ask someone who could certainly afford a brand new pair of boots for Alexis. She waited for hours at the Tocopilla Town Hall but eventually, the mayor welcomed her into his very nice office and asked how he could help.

'Sir, my son is Alexis Alejandro Sánchez – he is the star player for the Club Arauco de Tocopilla youth team.'

Martina paused and the mayor nodded; like everyone else in the area, he had heard about Alexis's talent. In the recent Under-14s tournament, Alexis had scored eight goals in one game. The people of Tocopilla were starting to call him *El Niño Maravilla* – 'The Wonder Boy'.

'Alexis needs a pair of football boots but I'm afraid we just don't have the money to pay for them. I don't know what else to do so I've come here to ask if we could perhaps have a loan or a grant to buy them. I would pay back the money as soon as I could, I promise.'

There was silence for a minute as the mayor thought about the problem. 'Please leave this with me and I will see what I can do. It won't be easy but we need to do what we can to help our brightest youngsters.'

Martina breathed a sigh of relief. Perhaps nothing would happen but at least there was still hope. 'Thank you, sir. It just breaks my heart to know that he is so good but I can't afford to give him what he needs.'

As the end of the month got closer, Alexis began to ask his mum about the boots again. Martina had heard nothing from the mayor but she didn't want to upset her son until she had to. Instead she prayed and told him to wait.

'Please be patient, Alexis. I'm working on it and we agreed that I would have until the first day of September.'

Martina could see that her son now expected her to fail. But just as she too began to give up hope, something magical happened.

It was ten o'clock at night and Marjorie, Humberto and Alexis were playing a card game before bedtime. Martina was sewing yet another patch on to the knee of a pair of Alexis's trousers when there was a knock at the door. Always full of energy, Alexis was the first to answer it.

'Is this the Sánchez household?' A man with a big moustache asked him. Alexis could see his delivery van out in the street.

'Yes.'

'Good, I have a package for Mr Alexis Alejandro

Sánchez,' the man said, reading off his clip-
board.

'That's me!' Alexis shouted. This was exciting; he
had never had a delivery before. What could it be?

'Here you go, young man,' he said, handing over a
rectangular box.

Alexis thanked him and ran inside to open it. The
family gathered around him to watch. Looking at the
box, Martina suddenly realised what this must be.

'FOOTBALL BOOTS! Wow Mum, these are
amazing – you're the best!'

She had never seen Alexis look so happy. They
were the most beautiful boots he had ever seen –
brand new Reeboks in classic black with the logos in
silver and some gold trim around the edges. He ran
over and gave his mum the biggest hug he had ever
given anyone. Martina stared in shock at the boots,
and said a silent thank you to the Mayor of Tocopilla.

It was usually time for Alexis to go to bed but he
had his new football boots on. There was no way he
could sleep right now, so he went out into the street
with Humberto to pass the ball around. The Reeboks

were a perfect fit and he loved the feel of kicking the ball with them. He could tell that his shooting would be much more powerful now. He would clean them every day to get rid of all the dirt and dust.

'Humberto, there's no stopping me now,' Alexis said as he looked down at his feet and smiled. 'This is it!'

'Alexis, time for bed!' Martina shouted out to him a few minutes later. 'And make sure you take those boots off before you get into bed.'

Alexis was usually a good son but for once he disobeyed his mother. He wasn't ready to take his new boots off just yet.

CHAPTER 7

THE NUMBER 10 ROLE

The coach Juan Segovia blew his whistle and the boys stopped taking shots and ran to where he stood at the halfway line. There was a lot of noise and excitement because it was time to start the first football practice of the year. It was a big day for everyone.

'Settle down, kids! Come on, listen! Welcome to the new season. We've got some really good players this year and if we get things right, we can win the league. I'm sure of it. There are twenty of you here today and I'm looking to pick a squad of fifteen. So work hard and impress me!'

With that, Mr Segovia began the warm-up. After

a set of stretches to loosen up the muscles, they did lots of short sprints. With or without a ball at his feet, Alexis loved to run. He was the quickest boy there and as everyone else slowed down and then gave up, Alexis just kept going until he was told to stop.

'Very good, Alexis,' Mr Segovia shouted. 'But save some energy for the rest of the practice!'

Alexis smiled; he had plenty of energy left. He was hardly sweating.

Next, the players were divided into four groups of five for some passing exercises. After showing them what he wanted, Mr Segovia slowly walked around the pitch, watching the different groups and offering advice.

'Take your time, Pablo!'

'Juan, get your head up earlier – look at who you're passing to!'

Alexis was calm and focused. In his new boots, he made sure that his first touch was perfect to control the ball, and that his pass was accurate and not too powerful. These were the boys that Alexis played with every day at *Cancha Lazareto* so he knew which foot they preferred to receive the pass with. He was determined to get everything just right for his new coach.

In the one-on-one exercise, Alexis was paired with Gonzalo, the best defender in Tocopilla. He was the only one who could ever keep *Dilla* quiet. On his first attempt, Alexis attacked with pace and quick feet but Gonzalo tackled him. Alexis could see Mr Segovia watching; he needed to do better than that. On this second attempt he took his time, kept it simple and used his brain. As he approached Gonzalo, he moved the ball towards the defender's weaker side. As Gonzalo adjusted his feet, Alexis quickly moved it back onto his right foot and took it past him. 'That's better,' Alexis said to himself.

'Very good!' Mr Segovia shouted.

The first practice of the season finished with a big match, Ten versus ten. Alexis started the match as his team's striker, the position that his hero Marcelo Salas played. He scored one goal but hit his next couple of shots over the bar. He was getting frustrated because his teammates were finding it hard to get the ball up to him. Alexis hated not being involved in everything.

Luckily, Mr Segovia had an idea. 'Darío, take Alexis's position – Alexis, play a little deeper just in front of the midfield!'

Mr Segovia knew that Alexis could score goals but he was sure that striker wasn't his best position. It was a waste of his incredible talent. For him, Alexis was a born *puntero*, a Number 10 like Diego Maradona. His shooting was good but he was more of a creator than a goalscorer.

Straight away, Alexis got on the ball and took control of the game. When his teammates won possession, they fed the ball to him and he found the killer pass for someone else to score. If there were no options ahead of him, he would dribble past opponents until a space opened up. Alexis loved his new freedom and used his energy to run from the left to the middle and then to the right. The defenders just couldn't keep up with his movement.

'I've got no chance now!' Gonzalo moaned as he tried to follow Alexis around the pitch.

Mr Segovia was very pleased with his decision. 'Brilliant stuff – Alexis, that's your position from now on.' He was watching a very special talent, the best player that he had ever coached. He would do everything he could to develop this boy's skills.

With Alexis in the *puntero* role, the Escuela Bernardo O'Higgins Riquelme E-10 team was unstoppable. Opponents would tell a player to man-mark Alexis but he was just too clever and too gifted. He wasn't very tall but he was strong enough to compete with much bigger players. Unlike some skilful attackers, Alexis never stopped working hard for the team. He chased opponents and made sure that he was always available for the pass. They kicked and fouled him but Alexis just kept creating great chances for his teammates. And E-10 just kept winning.

By now everyone in the region knew about *El Niño Maravilla*. Every week, important scouts came to watch him play but the pressure didn't bother Alexis; he had complete faith in his talent and loved a challenge. O'Higgins, a big club in Rancagua in central Chile, tried to sign him but he wasn't ready to go so far from home. He had a long way to go but he was pleased to be making a name for himself. The question everyone was asking was: just how good could he become? Alexis was very confident about the answer.

'I'm going to get to the top. I'm going to be one of the best players in the world.'

CHAPTER 8

SCOUTED

Roberto Spicto smiled to himself and waited for
the match to end. It had been a good day for
him and hopefully it would be a good day for
his football club, Cobreloa, too. As youth team
manager, his job was not only to develop the
players at the club but also to find new talent.
Roberto often travelled the full length of Chile to
watch young stars but this time it had been a nice
simple two-hour drive. His hopes had been high
ever since the previous week, when the general
manager of the Club Arauco de Tocopilla youth
team had called him.

'Roberto, I have a great player here who you need

to come and watch. Honestly, he's far and away the best we've ever had.'

It wasn't every day that a football coach called him to talk with such excitement about one of his own players. Roberto decided it was definitely worth a trip to see this kid in action as soon as possible.

Roberto met Rodolfo, the Tocopilla manager, before the match and he pointed out Alexis, the star of his team. 'That's the one you're here to watch. Trust me: you're looking at the future captain of Chile.'

Roberto's first thought was that the kid looked quite small. However, as he joked around with his teammates, he could see that Alexis was strong enough to make up for his lack of height. As he waited for the game to kick off, he balanced the ball on the back of his neck and then flicked it on to his right foot and then his left with great control. Roberto could see that he had lots of skill and he liked that Alexis was having fun. That was very important at such a young age.

After two minutes, Roberto knew that he owed

Rodolfo a very big favour. Alexis was playing as an attacking midfielder and he was running the game. This was a player that Cobreloa really needed to sign. Every time Alexis got the ball, he looked like he would do something magical – a great pass, a brilliant trick, or a powerful shot. Roberto had never seen a fourteen-year-old play with such personality and spirit. It was so exciting to watch someone this special.

At the final whistle, Roberto ran over to speak to the Tocopilla manager. As he approached, Rodolfo laughed and waved his finger. 'I told you, didn't I? And that wasn't even one of his best matches.'

'Yes, you were right! He's sensational. Can I talk to him?'

Rodolfo called out to Alexis, and the boy came running over. He was barely even sweating after playing a whole match. That was impressive.

'Alexis, this is Roberto. He's the youth team coach for Cobreloa. Have you heard of Cobreloa?'

Alexis nodded shyly and shook Roberto's hand. It was good to see that he was a polite boy.

'It's nice to meet you, Alexis. You played really well today – I see a very bright future for you. We've got an excellent youth system at Cobreloa, with lots of experienced, older players to help you develop. Would you be interested in coming to train with us?'

'That would be amazing!' Alexis replied with a massive grin on his face.

'Great, well we could bring you over next week to see if you like it. Does that sound good?'

'Yes please!'

Alexis had never felt so excited as he arrived at the Cobreloa training ground. It wasn't that big compared to the clubs he would go on to play for, but it was a huge step-up from the *Cancha Lazareto* he was used to. He had been dreaming about this day ever since Roberto invited him. Some nights he dreamt that he played the best game of his life and they moved him straight to the first team; other nights, he dreamt that he forgot all of his kit, or got a really bad injury. He was determined to do well. He thought of it as an opportunity, rather than a trial. He was confident in his talent.

'Welcome, Alexis,' Roberto said, shaking his hand. 'Great to see you again!' He introduced Alexis to the other coaches, handed him a Cobreloa shirt and told him to go out and play. Alexis didn't need to be told twice. By now he was used to training exercises; he understood that they were important for improving players, even if it was more fun to just play a real game instead. The drills at Cobreloa were much harder than anything he'd done before but Alexis was a fast learner.

'Very good!' Roberto said to him as he walked around the pitch, watching each of the groups. Alexis was pleased that he was doing well but he was looking forward to the match at the end. That was where he would really be able to impress.

It took Alexis a little while to get the ball but when he did, he was unstoppable. The Cobreloa youth players were very good but they were no match for him. Roberto could hardly contain his excitement as Alexis ran at the defence with that unique style of his. With the little jumps, turns and stepovers, he looked like he was dancing. But not only did it look amazing, it also created goals – and lots of them. Alexis's team won easily, and he was already one of the boys.

By the end of the match, Roberto had the contract ready for Alexis to sign.

CHAPTER 9

EARLY DAYS AT COBRELOA

'Mum, I have some big news!' Alexis shouted as he ran through the front door. Martina was in the kitchen preparing dinner. She knew her son's news would be about football; it was all he ever talked about.

'Cobreloa have offered me a contract!' Alexis said, throwing his arms around his mum. With all of the scouts coming to watch him play, he had been desperately hoping that a professional club would sign him. Cobreloa played in Chile's top league, the Primera Division. It was a massive opportunity for him.

'Wait a minute – does that mean you have to move to Calama?' Martina asked. Calama was nearly one hundred miles east of Tocopilla. If Alexis accepted the deal, he would have to leave his hometown behind. She wasn't sure that her son, still just sixteen years old, was ready for that.

'Yes, but that's not that far away,' Alexis replied. 'I'd be able to come back every few weeks, and I'd be able to send you some of my wages.'

It was true that the money would be useful but Martina was worried. Her son had only left Tocopilla a couple of times in his life. Did Alexis know how to do his own washing? Did he know how to cook? Could he look after himself? But she knew there was no point arguing with Alexis; he would get his own way and at sixteen, it was time for him to become more independent.

It was the happiest moment of Alexis's life so far. He had worked really hard on improving his game and now his reward was a place in the youth team of one of Chile's biggest teams. His favourite team was Universidad de Chile, Marcelo Salas's team, but he didn't mind who he played for as long as he was playing professional football. And this was just the start – his dream was eventually to play for one of the biggest clubs in Europe, in Italy, Spain or England.

Leaving home for the first time, Alexis was glad to find that Calama wasn't too different from Tocopilla. It was bigger and there was less poverty but it was still a mining area in Chile's northern, desert region. There was an airport and a large business district, but the dry air and dust made Alexis feel at home.

Cobreloa's youth players were placed with families in the city, where they would be cooked for and looked after. Alexis was quite nervous as he stood outside his new home. It looked much nicer and bigger than his house in Tocopilla. There were flowers in the front garden rather than broken toys, and there was no high fence to keep out stray dogs. Taking a deep breath, he knocked on the front door.

'Hello Alexis! Welcome to our home,' the man greeted him, shaking his hand and taking his small suitcase of belongings. 'I'm Luis, this is my wife Ana and these are our daughters, Barbara and Andrea.'

Alexis was usually very confident when meeting new people but suddenly he felt shy. The Astorga family were really friendly but everything felt new and strange for him. Luis took him around the house and showed him his bedroom at the back of the building. Alexis had never had a room of his own; in Tocopilla, he had shared a small space with his brother Humberto.

'Will this be okay for you?' Luis asked and Alexis just nodded and smiled.

Over dinner, they talked about football. Luis was a massive Cobreloa fan and went to all of the home games. He proudly showed Alexis his orange shirt and orange scarf. He was very excited to have a future star in the family.

'So what position do you play? Let me guess – you're a striker, the new Salas?'

Alexis smiled at the mention of his hero. 'No, I'm a *puntero* or a winger. I'm very fast and skilful.'

'We like skilful players in Calama. In a year or two, we'll all be wearing "Alexis" shirts!' Luis joked.

Alexis got on really well with his new second family. When he wasn't training and playing matches, he was working in the garden with Luis

or watching TV with his new sisters, Barbara and
Andrea. Alexis liked to be useful and Luis loved
having a 'new son'.

'How is it going with the Desert Foxes?' Luis
asked him as they chopped wood for the stove.
Zorros del Desierto was the club nickname. 'Do the
senior players talk to you and help you to improve?'

'Yes, they're great. There are lots of experienced
guys who have played for really big teams. They've
got lots of advice for us youngsters.'

From his very first day at Cobreloa, his new
teammates had welcomed him warmly, even when
he admitted that he was a Universidad de Chile
supporter.

'You should keep that quiet!' Nelson Tapia told
him with a smile on his face. 'We don't care but the
fans won't be happy if they hear that!'

It didn't take the Cobreloa players and coaches
long to see that Alexis was a player with a really
bright future. He always gave one hundred per
cent on the training ground and everyone was very
impressed with his attitude. They encouraged him to

try new things but always told him if he was doing too many tricks.

'That's enough, Alexis!' Nelson shouted, giving him a cheeky kick on the ankle. 'You're just showing off now; make sure that your skills are productive. It's pointless unless you're creating goals.'

Alexis loved the challenge of training with such experienced professionals. There were a lot of talented young footballers at Cobreloa and everyone was improving really quickly. In the youth team, Alexis had Charles Aránguiz behind him in midfield and Eduardo Vargas ahead of him up front. They were a fantastic and exciting side.

Alexis listened carefully to all advice and learned quickly from his mistakes. And it wasn't just on the football pitch where his teammates were helping him. Nelson gave him a brand new pair of Nike football boots when his Reeboks finally broke. They were a size too big but they looked great and he was really grateful to have them. The Cobreloa players were also teaching him life skills like looking after money, folding clothes and making pizzas and salads.

Alexis was growing up fast and his mum would be proud of him.

'Mum, you won't believe it but I'm becoming a pretty good chef!' he told Martina excitedly on the phone. 'My teammates put me in charge of the barbeque last night and they said it was some of the best meat they'd ever had!'

Alexis really missed his friends and family back in Tocopilla but he was pleased with the progress he was making at Cobreloa. He was sure that he would be moving up to the first team very soon.

CHAPTER 10

PLAYING WITH
THE BIG BOYS

'Alexis, we've been keeping an eye on you for a while,' Cobreloa manager Nelson Acosta said.

They were sitting in his office and Alexis was shaking with nerves. Nelson had managed the Chilean national team at the 1998 World Cup in France, and could be a very scary man. Had Alexis done something wrong? Was he in trouble?

'We've decided that you're ready to make the step up to the senior team,' the manager went on. 'Do *you* think you're ready?'

Alexis's heart was beating so fast that he could barely speak. 'Yes, I'm definitely ready! I've been working really hard, Coach. You won't regret this!'

He had always been tough for his size but Alexis had added lots of muscle and now looked like a man rather than a boy. The extra power had made him even quicker and even more dangerous in attack. He was so happy that his improvement had been noticed. He was desperate to start playing in the *Campeonato Nacional*, the top Chilean league.

'Mum, they're promoting me to the first team!' Alexis shouted down the phone.

'That's brilliant, well done!' Martina replied, passing the great news on to Humberto and Marjorie. She was so proud of her son.

The Astorga family was equally pleased. Luis couldn't wait to watch Alexis make his Cobreloa debut. 'Look, I have my "Alexis" shirt ready,' he said, holding up his new orange item of clothing.

That debut came at home against Deportes Temuco, a team from the south of Chile. As soon as Alexis knew he was in the matchday squad, he called his mum and she started making plans for the journey to Calama. There was no way that she would miss the match. Alexis hardly ever felt nervous before a game, but this wasn't just any game. A dry wind was blowing through the *Estadio Zorros del Desierto* as Alexis did his pre-match stretches. He looked up into the stands and saw his mum sitting there with Luis, Ana, Barbara and Andrea. He waved at them and then focused on the game.

As he came out on to the pitch for kick-off in his club tracksuit, the noise was incredible. Alexis was still only sixteen years old but this was what he was born to do. He was one of the substitutes and if he came on, he would become one of Cobreloa's youngest ever players. It was hard to believe that he was now playing for the first team, alongside players that he really looked up to. His dream was already coming true.

Alexis found it hard to watch the game from the bench. He kept shifting around in his seat and fiddling with the zip on his jacket. He just wanted to get on the pitch and show everyone what he could do.

'How many minutes left?' he asked Italo

Traverso, the Cobreloa fitness coach, early in the second half.

'About three minutes less than last time you asked. Calm down!' he replied.

It was a really close game and the teams were tied at 4–4. With twenty minutes to go, the coach told Alexis to warm up. He was finally coming on. He wasn't nervous anymore; he couldn't wait. This was his big day and he was going to enjoy every minute of it. He replaced Daniel Pérez on the right wing. The Temuco team looked at the small, young Cobreloa substitute and thought, 'He doesn't look ready for this. He's just a kid.'

But as soon as he entered the field, Alexis changed the game with his energy and skill. The fans cheered loudly as he attacked at defenders, faking to go one way and then going the other. They had no idea what he was going to do next. He had no fear of making mistakes because he believed that he was good enough to do anything. He never stopped running and calling for the ball. The opponents didn't believe that he could keep this pace up for the rest of the game but his own teammates knew that he could. The Temuco coach told one of their players to man-mark Alexis but it made no difference.

'Wow, this kid is special,' Nelson Acosta said to his assistant sat next to him on the bench. He was very pleased with his decision to bring Alexis on. He was going to win the game for them.

'He's from another planet!' Boris González said to himself as he watched his teammate win the ball back and sprint up the field towards goal.

Alexis didn't score but he did set up Diego Guidi to win the game for Cobreloa with just four minutes to go. Alexis celebrated the goal like it was his own; he was now a big part of the team and it was the best feeling in the world. At the final whistle, all of his teammates congratulated him on an amazing debut.

'That was unbelievable! I've never seen anything like it,' Nelson Tapia shouted as they made their way off the pitch. 'You played like you do on the training pitch – weren't you nervous before your first game?'

Alexis shook his head – he wasn't nervous because he knew he was ready. He would never forget this day, and he would enjoy his success for one night, but then it was back to the training ground – he was already looking ahead to the next match. He wanted to be in the starting eleven and show what he could do over the full ninety minutes.

Watching the game, Martina had never been so proud in all her life. Her son was now a Cobreloa hero and one of the nation's brightest young talents. After giving him a massive hug, she ran to Nelson Acosta and gave him one too. She was crying tears of joy.

'Thank you!' she said to the Cobreloa manager. 'Thank you for showing such faith in my son!'

CHAPTER 11

NEXT STEPS TO GREATNESS

Things were going really well for Alexis. Since
his amazing debut, he had played in every game
for Cobreloa and he was getting better and better.
Wearing the Number 7 shirt, Alexis was the new fan
favourite. They cheered each step over he did and
each defender he dribbled past.

'You've only been playing for a month and they
already love you more than me!' Nelson Tapia joked
after another victory. Alexis loved to go over to the
Cobreloa fans after each game and clap and wave
to them. He was living his dream and he wanted to
say thank you to the people who supported him. He
was always friendly and polite when he met fans on

the streets of Calama too. He stopped to talk, sign autographs and have photos taken.

In training, there were two things that Alexis was working really hard to perfect – his crossing from the wing and his shooting. He was desperate to get his first goal for Cobreloa.

'I'm an attacker and I'm creating lots of goals but I need to score them too,' he told Humberto on the phone.

'Don't worry!' replied his brother back in Tocopilla, who proudly watched every game he could. 'You're only sixteen – the goals will come soon, I'm sure.'

Humberto was right – Alexis was always keen to improve. Against Concepción, he scored and it was the best feeling of his life. He ran towards the fans behind the goal, pointing at them. He had never heard so much noise in the stadium. As his teammates jumped on him to celebrate, he pointed to the sky to thank God for everything. He had a lot to be thankful for.

Alexis's goal meant that Cobreloa would play in the

Copa Libertadores, the biggest tournament in Latin American football. He was so excited – he would be one of the youngest players ever to play in the competition. He would be able to test himself against famous teams like Boca Juniors and River Plate from Argentina, and – from Brazil – Pele's old team Santos. And the winner of that tournament would play in the FIFA Club World Championship against teams like Barcelona, Real Madrid and Manchester United. Cobreloa were not expected to win but even so, Alexis couldn't wait for the challenge.

The good news just kept coming. Alexis rang his mother.

'Are you ready to hear something brilliant?' he said. 'I've been invited to train with the Chile national team!'

Martina screamed with joy. Her son would be playing for his country. 'Well done, Alexis!' She ran out of the house to share the news with the whole of Tocopilla.

Alexis was a little nervous to be training with such excellent players but he was determined to impress.

And at least he knew the manager very well –
Nelson Acosta, his old coach at Cobreloa.

'Hello, stranger!' Nelson Acosta said as he arrived,
giving him a big hug.

The most exciting part for Alexis was the chance
to meet his hero, Chile's greatest ever striker,
Marcelo Salas, and to play alongside him.

'Great to meet you,' Marcelo said, shaking his
hand. 'I've heard a lot about you from my friends
at Cobreloa. They say that one day you're going to
break my goalscoring record for Chile!'

Alexis laughed but didn't know what to say. He
was star-struck for the first time in his life. He would
never forget this moment.

In just one week, Alexis learnt so much. Marcelo
had lots of advice for him about shooting and about
dealing with the pressure of being a star player.
'You're lucky to have such good teammates – they'll
look after you. Soon, teams will start using two or
three defenders to stop you. That will be difficult.
You won't have so much space and you'll need to
find new ways to create chances.'

Alexis listened carefully to everything that was said to him. He wanted to remember every little piece of guidance. He knew that he would need them all if he was to become one of the best players in the world.

But just when he thought the only way was up, Alexis got some bad news. His mum had been caught selling fish without a licence. There was a big fine to pay and the Sánchez family couldn't afford it.

'Son, I'm so sorry to ask but is there anything you can do?' Martina asked in tears. 'Perhaps Cobreloa could help?'

Alexis had had to grow up fast when he left home and he was determined to protect his family now that he could. 'Don't worry, mum. I'll speak to my teammates. I'll take care of this.'

'Have you got an agent yet?' Nelson Tapia asked when Alexis spoke to him. He shook his head; he hadn't even thought about that.

'Well, that's what you need to do – you're the biggest young talent in Chile. There are hundreds who would love to look after you. I'll put you in touch with a good one.'

Fernando Felicevich didn't dress like a tough businessman, liked to laugh and loved football. Alexis felt very comfortable with him, and the two got on really well straight away.

'Look, you're one of the top ten young players in South America now – I hope you realise that!' said Fernando. 'Soon, European clubs will hear about you and then there will be lots of big offers. You need someone who can give you good advice about really important decisions. I'd love to help you if you'd like me to.'

Alexis was impressed, and he already needed help with making one particular decision. He explained his mum's predicament. 'No problem,' Fernando replied calmly. 'I can get that sorted. If we sign this contract right now, I'll get your mum's fine paid today!'

They shook hands, and Alexis went to tell his mum the good news. Having an agent was a big step but it felt good to have people around him that he

could trust, people who could help him to get to the
very top.

CHAPTER 12

INTEREST FROM ITALY

Fernando was right; European clubs were quickly learning about Alexis's talent. At top Italian club Udinese Calcio, Fabrizio Larini sat in a meeting with his team of scouts. The club's scouting centre received lots of performance tapes of great young players from all over the world. Their task was to review all of them and pick out the very best. It was a really fun job but it was always difficult to predict who would be a future superstar, and who would fade.

'So who has impressed you in the videos you've watched this week?' he asked from the head of the table.

'This kid Alexis Sánchez is the best we've seen in months,' replied one scout, Juan, pressing play on the video on the big screen. They all watched as Alexis ran rings around his opponents and scored a wonder goal. 'He plays anywhere in attack and he's got everything,' Juan went on, 'skill, pace, vision and desire.'

Fabrizio was impressed by what he saw. 'Very good indeed – what club does he play for?'

'Cobreloa in Northern Chile.'

'Okay, well we need to go and watch him live!'

Fabrizio sent a couple of Udinese's South American scouts to Cobreloa straight away. They said, 'We've seen the videos but we want to know if Alexis Sánchez is really *that* good!'

Two matches and two standing ovations later, the scouts confirmed that he really was, telling Fabrizio: 'You have to sign him quickly! He's so exciting to watch and he never stops running. He's a little selfish at times but he causes so much damage. Plus, he's calm under pressure and very strong for a creative player. He really is The Wonder Boy!'

'And you think he can get even better?'

'The sky's the limit for Alexis – he could be the next Ronaldinho or Zidane!'

After such high praise, Fabrizio's mind was made up. His team had watched all of Alexis's videos over and over again and they were sure that this was a very special player. When he heard that Manchester United were also interested in signing Alexis, Fabrizio knew it was time to make his move.

Alexis jumped for joy at the news that Udinese wanted to buy him. 'I've always dreamed of playing in Serie A!' he told his teammates excitedly. Now it was coming true and only just over a year after making his senior debut. He was very proud of his Cobreloa record – twelve goals in fifty games was brilliant for a teenager. Alexis would be following in the footsteps of Chilean legends Iván Zamorano and his personal hero, Marcelo Salas. It was hard to believe, but he had always believed in his talent, and so had his family.

'Congratulations, that's brilliant news!' Martina

screamed when he told her on the phone. 'My son will be a top player in Italy!' Alexis was already famous in Tocopilla but now he was the talk of the whole city. Everyone was so proud of how well their local boy was doing.

After a few days of talks with Cobreloa, Udinese bought Alexis for £1.7 million. It was a lot of money to pay for an unknown seventeen-year-old but Fabrizio knew that it was worth the risk. In a few years, they would have one of the world's best attackers in their team.

For Alexis, things just kept getting better and better. He had trained with the Chilean national team before but this time his old Cobreloa coach Nelson Acosta named him on the bench for Chile's friendly match against New Zealand. Alexis couldn't stop smiling – it was unbelievable how quickly his career was moving forward. He had signed for a big European club and now, hopefully, he would become a Chilean international. Martina was the first person he told.

'Nothing surprises me anymore!' she told her son,

laughing. 'Every time you call me, you have amazing news to share.'

Alexis hated being a substitute, though. He wanted to be out on the pitch playing football and he found it impossible to just sit still and watch the action, which was why he very rarely watched football on TV. Eventually, with nearly one-third of the New Zealand game left, he came on for his Chilean debut and became their youngest ever international player. It was the proudest moment of his life to represent his country.

'That was just the start,' Alexis panted at the final whistle. 'I'm going to get over a hundred caps!'

Back in club football, the big question was whether or not Alexis was ready for the move to Europe yet. The Chilean season wasn't over and Fabrizio had seen many young players struggle with the culture shock of being so far from home. He wanted to protect Udinese's new talent as much as possible. Luckily, Alexis received a phone call that made the decision much easier.

'Hi Alexis, this is Claudio Borghi.'

Claudio paused, as if to suggest that Alexis should recognise the name, but he didn't. Alexis was relaxing with his family and the call had taken him completely by surprise. Was Claudio an agent, or a scout perhaps?

'Sorry, who is this?'

There was another pause, before the caller said: 'I'm Claudio Borghi, the manager of Colo-Colo.'

Alexis felt very embarrassed – how had he forgotten the name of the South American Coach of the Year? 'I'm really sorry about that. How can I help?'

'I'm calling to see if you'd be interested in joining our team. We'd really love to have you here!'

Alexis was speechless – it was a real honour to be wanted by the biggest club in Chile, but he had already signed for Udinese. In his head, he was already looking forward to playing in front of massive crowds in Italy but he was also worried about being homesick. Moving to Italy was a really big step at his age with so little life experience.

What could he do? He decided to tell Fabrizio about Claudio's offer.

Fabrizio was impressed by Alexis's honesty and maturity. Youngsters often wanted to rush their rise to the top. This, however, was a sensible option – Alexis would be able to build up slowly to bigger and bigger challenges. Fabrizio felt that a loan deal suited everyone.

'At Udinese we believe in looking after our players properly,' he explained over coffee in Calama. 'You're still very young and we believe players develop best in an environment where they're comfortable. By playing at Colo-Colo for one season, you'll be able to stay in Chile and you'll also be playing against the other best teams in South America in the Copa Libertadores.'

Alexis was sorry to be leaving Cobreloa behind. He had a lot of love for the club, the players and the fans. They had really helped him to grow up and he owed them a lot. Alexis wouldn't be playing European football just yet but he would be playing for Chile's most successful club, and he would be moving to Santiago, the country's big capital city. He couldn't wait for his next adventure.

CHAPTER 13

CHAMPION OF CHILE

Claudio Borghi couldn't stop smiling when he heard that Alexis would join Colo-Colo on loan for the season. He was exactly the kind of exciting, attacking player that his team needed. Colo-Colo had won the *Torneo Apertura*, the first half of the Chilean football season, but they were struggling to continue their form in the second half, the *Torneo Clausura*. 'What a lovely present this is!' Claudio told his staff.

Alexis was really impressed by the Colo-Colo squad. Just like at Cobreloa, there was a really good mix of more experienced players and younger talent but Arturo Vidal, Humberto Suazo and Matías Fernández were some of the best players he'd ever played with. He knew that he'd have to play really well to break into the starting line-up. But once they were all used to playing with each other, he was sure that they would be unstoppable.

Alexis's debut for Colo-Colo ended in a draw. It was an amazing feeling to hear the fans chanting his name but he was disappointed not to create a winning goal for his new team.

'I played quite well but I needed to start *really* well!' he told his brother Humberto. 'I want to play every minute of every game but there are lots of good attackers here and only three can start each match.'

Alexis was desperate to become a fan favourite straight away but it took a little while for him to settle in. When he turned up for his first day of training, the club presented him with a nice box of cookies. Alexis didn't know what to say – he'd never been given gifts like that. For a shy boy from Tocopilla, life in Santiago was very different. He found it hard to get used to all of the traffic, pollution, noise and money in the capital city, when his heart was still back in his home town. With his first wages, he paid for a new house to be built for his mum and sister.

'Mum, I told you that I when I became a professional footballer I would look after you,' Alexis said, as Martina broke down in tears at the news. 'When we were young, you worked so hard to look after us. But you don't need to work anymore – I'll look after you now.'

Four months after his arrival at Colo-Colo, Alexis was selected for the *Superclásico*, the massive derby match against Universidad de Chile. It was the biggest game in Chilean football, and to qualify for the *Clausura* play-offs they needed three points. The atmosphere in the *Estadio Monumental David Arellano* was incredible. Alexis had never heard so much noise in a football stadium but he wasn't nervous at all; he enjoyed this kind of pressure.

Alexis had grown up as a Universidad de Chile fan because that was the team that his idol Marcelo Salas played for. Salas was still a Universidad de Chile player and would be playing against Alexis today.

However, none of this really crossed the seventeen-year-old's mind – he was just determined to be the Colo-Colo hero. With half an hour to go, the score was 1–1. Álvaro Ormeño won the ball on the right and ran forward. Alexis made a great run into the Universidad de Chile penalty area and Álvaro passed it through to him. Instead of controlling the ball, Alexis decided to strike it straight away and his shot deflected off the defender and past the goalkeeper. *Gooooooooooaaaaaaaaaaaaaaaaaalllllllllllllll!*

It was Alexis's first for Colo-Colo and he ran towards the home fans to celebrate. There was nothing quite like the feeling of scoring a goal. His teammates quickly came over to congratulate him. Colo-Colo won 4–2 and the after-match party went on for hours.

With Alexis as a key starter in attack, Colo-Colo went on to win the *Torneo Clausura*. It was the club's twenty-fifth title but it was his first professional trophy – and he enjoyed every second of it.

'This is why I became a footballer,' Alexis told Arturo Vidal as they celebrated on the pitch after victory in the final. 'I love winning and I want to be the best!'

Colo-Colo also won the next *Torneo Apertura*. It completed a great year for Alexis and the club. He hadn't scored as many goals as he'd wanted to, but playing in a brilliant team, he had improved in many other areas. With every game, he got better at beating defenders and finding the space he needed to create his magic.

When the season ended, Alexis headed off to the Under-20 World Cup in Canada with Arturo. They had both made a few appearances for the senior team but Chile wanted their group of very talented youngsters to get as much experience as possible.

'We've got a really good chance of winning this,' Alexis told the squad when they arrived. Although he was one of the younger players, he had played the most games at the highest level and so his teammates looked up to him. 'If we play well as a team, we can beat anyone!'

Chile topped their group, with Alexis and Arturo both scoring. In the knock-out rounds, they beat

Portugal and Nigeria to set up a semi-final against
tournament favourites, Argentina, who had Ángel Di
María and Sergio Agüero in their team. Alexis knew
it would be a really difficult match but he always
stayed positive. If you didn't believe you could win,
there was no way that you would win.

Chile lost to Argentina but then still beat Austria
to take third place. The tournament had been a real
success for Chile and a good learning experience for
Alexis. There was still a lot of work to do but he had
certainly added to his growing reputation.

'We've got a great group of young players at the
moment – they're calling us a golden generation,'
Alexis said to Arturo on their way home. 'If we keep
playing together, imagine how good we could be in
five years' time!'

Where next? That was the question on Alexis's
mind as he returned to Santiago. He was pretty
sure that he wouldn't be returning to Colo-Colo
for another season but would Udinese think he
was ready to come to Italy? His Chilean teammate
Mauricio Isla was already there and could help him

settle in. He felt ready but he trusted the club to do what was best for him. In the end, Fabrizio decided that another season in South America would be best.

'Alexis, we've received an offer from River Plate,' he told him on the phone during the July break. 'They want to take you on loan for next season and we think it's a really good idea.'

Alexis was happy to agree – River Plate were one of the biggest clubs in South America – and so, before the big move to Italy, there would be a smaller move to Buenos Aires, in Argentina.

CHAPTER 14

AN ARGENTINIAN EDUCATION

'Welcome to River Plate,' the manager Daniel Passarella said, shaking Alexis's hand.

Alexis was too nervous to reply; Passarella was a footballing legend, the captain of Argentina's 1978 World Cup-winning team. It was one thing playing for Colo-Colo, Chile's biggest club, but playing for River Plate was an even bigger honour and an even bigger challenge. The club had won the Argentinian league a record thirty-five times and finished runners-up thirty times. They had also won lots of international trophies with superstar players like Hernan Crespo and Alexis's hero Marcelo Salas.

However, when Alexis joined on loan, River Plate

hadn't won a trophy in three years. They had former Argentinian international Ariel Ortega in the squad but otherwise were short on quality and talent. They hoped that Alexis would make a big difference. Everyone had heard about him and the positive comparisons with Argentinian superstar Lionel Messi. The pressure was on.

'It's great to have you here,' Ariel told him at his first training session. He was impressed by how hard Alexis was working. Sometimes really gifted players could be very lazy, but not Alexis. 'This is a great club and a great league. I just hope you're ready for the defenders!'

Argentinian football was famous for its tough tackling. Skilful players had to deal with kicks, shirt-pulls, pushes and elbows. 'Don't worry about me – I can handle it!' Alexis replied with confidence.

'*Chileeeno! Chileeeno!*' the River Plate fans chanted as Alexis ran out for his debut. The atmosphere was even better than at Colo-Colo. Alexis couldn't believe it. He could remember watching Salas playing for River Plate on TV and hearing the incredible noise. Now it was his turn. Every time he got the ball, the crowd cheered and cheered as he dribbled at defenders and fooled them with his many tricks. But as Ariel had warned him, opposition defenders were soon doing anything to stop him. Alexis could usually see the bad tackles coming but he couldn't always avoid them.

'I'm not scared and I won't change the way I play!' Alexis told Ariel. He had just been to the club physio for treatment on his injured ankle. Alexis would need to rest it for at least a month and he wasn't happy about it. The Argentinian defenders were fouling him all the time and he was the one being punished for it. It wasn't fair.

'No, you should never change your style but it's about making the right decisions,' Ariel replied. As a young player, he had gone through the same problems and he was keen to pass on the advice that he had been given. 'You'll learn when to run with the ball and when to pass it.'

When they were on international duty together, Marcelo Salas told Alexis the same thing. 'When

you're young and skilful, defenders are going to hurt
you. Never give up on your style of play but you
have to be clever and get used to being beaten up!'

Alexis always listened to what his superstar
teammates said. He knew he still had a lot to learn
about making the most of his talent. He couldn't do
everything on his own and needed to be better about
passing and picking his runs.

New River Plate manager, Diego Simeone, was
also worried about protecting his young Chilean
attacker. 'You're still only nineteen years old and
we need to make sure you don't get a really serious
injury,' Diego told Alexis. 'I know you're determined
and that's great but we have to be careful.'

Another Argentinian had also taken Alexis under
his wing. Marcelo Bielsa, the new manager of Chile,
loved the way his star player attacked but he could
see ways to make him even better.

'Sometimes, the best thing is to get the ball and
run forward as fast as you can. But you need to get
your head up and think more,' Marcelo explained to
him in training, tapping his head again and again. He

was known as *Loco Bielsa* ('Crazy Bielsa') because of his love of tactical details. 'Is there a striker in the box for you to cross to? If not, what other options do you have? There's no shame in going backwards if it will later lead to a goal.'

Thanks to all of this advice, Alexis understood more and more about football. He came off the bench for River Plate in a few matches but Diego couldn't keep him out for long. He was too important to the team and he was the exciting player that all of the fans wanted to watch.

'They say you're more popular than Riquelme!' his teammates told him after reading a newspaper article. Alexis laughed; Juan Roman Riquelme was the star player for their massive rivals, Boca Juniors.

Alexis was improving with every game and, with Diego Buonanotte and Radamel Falcao, he formed a great attacking trio. Team spirit was really high and in 2008 River Plate won the *Torneo Clausura*, Alexis's second trophy in two years.

'Everywhere I go, I bring success!' Alexis

joked with his teammates after the last game of
the season. They had a great time together and
he would miss them a lot if he had to go. The
Argentinians in the squad made fun of his Chilean
accent but they loved having him around. And they
had introduced Alexis to *mate*, the local tea, which
he now drank every day.

'I've loved playing with you,' Radamel told his
strike partner. 'It's so much fun – when you get out
on that pitch, you're still a kid playing street football!'

Alexis was trying not to think about his future.
After a brilliant season, River Plate wanted to sign
him permanently and the Udinese general manager,
Franco Soldati, had given them a price – at least £17
million. Alexis was very happy to stay in Argentina,
but why didn't Udinese want him? The top clubs
in Europe were interested in him but his own club
seemed happy to let him leave.

'Maybe they think I'm not strong enough to play
in Italy,' he told his brother Humberto as he waited
for news, 'but it can't be any more physical than
Argentina!'

Finally, Alexis got the call he was waiting for. After two good seasons in South America, Udinese had decided that he was ready for Serie A.

CHAPTER 15

READY FOR SERIE A

'Alexis will be better than me.' That's what Marcelo Salas had said, and now Alexis was off to play in Italy, where Marcelo had played for Lazio and Juventus. Iván Zamorano had also done really well at Inter Milan, so there was a lot of expectation for this latest Chilean superstar. Countryman Mauricio Isla was there to welcome him. 'It's nice to see a friendly face!' Alexis said, with a big smile and a hug.

Alexis took the Number 11 shirt – he wanted everyone to know that he wasn't in Italy to be a substitute. This was his biggest step so far but he showed no fear. Udinese were one of the best teams in the league and would be playing in the UEFA

Cup again this season. The club had two of the best strikers in Serie A – Antonio Di Natale and Fabio Quagliarella – and Alexis's job would be to create lots of chances for them to score.

'The Wonder Boy has finally arrived!' Antonio joked as Alexis was introduced at training. 'Let's hope you're as good as they say you are.'

It didn't take long for Alexis to impress the star forward, not just with his ability but also his focus.

'You've got the skills of a juggler,...' Antonio said as he watched him practising his latest trick again and again and again until it was perfect, '...and the hunger of a wolf!'

Alexis loved walking around the city of Udine, looking at its beautiful old squares and palaces. The canals of Venice weren't far away either. It was quite a relaxed lifestyle that was more like Tocopilla or Calama than the busy capital cities of Santiago and Buenos Aires.

During his first season in Italy, Alexis was good but not spectacular. His first goal for the club wasn't a brilliant solo strike where he dribbled around the whole team. Instead, it was an ugly tap-in after running hard down the right wing to meet a cross from the left. His second goal however, two weeks later, was brilliant. He cut in from the left, went past two defenders and struck the ball powerfully into the bottom corner from thirty yards out.

Alexis's problem was that he couldn't yet do something that special in every game. Italian defenders were very good at keeping him quiet and blocking him.

'It takes time to get it right,' Antonio told him when he saw Alexis sitting alone in the dressing room. The newspapers had started to criticise his performances. 'Just keep working hard!'

Alexis was very glad to have good teammates who supported him through hard times. Against Bologna, he found his form again. He had been dangerous all game, but with less than a minute to go, the score was still 0–0. He ran forward with the ball, beat one defender and then hit a powerful left-foot shot past the goalkeeper. He was so excited to score the winning goal that he took his shirt off.

Alexis was learning a lot about tactics. As a young kid, he hadn't even known the positions on the pitch. Now in Italy he had to think about different formations and help the full-back behind him as well as the attackers ahead of him. He loved adding new areas to his game.

Alexis's second season at Udinese wasn't the great improvement that he'd hoped for. Antonio Di Natale was scoring goal after goal but he needed more support from his teammates, especially Alexis – who despite hard work just couldn't find the net.

'You worry too much!' Antonio told him. As club captain, he was always encouraging his teammates. 'Just keep creating goals for me. 2010 is going to be your year, I can tell.'

Antonio was right. In April of that year everything finally slotted into place. Alexis scored four goals in five games and was named Man of the Match against Roma in the Coppa Italia semi-final. In a 4–1 win against Siena, he scored one, set up one and won a penalty for another.

'None of them have been really good goals,' Alexis

said to Antonio, 'but suddenly I'm getting into the right place at the right time to score.'

Antonio smiled; as Serie A's top goalscorer, he knew all about that. 'Luck is crucial but it's also instinct. You're learning to hunt for goals!'

Overall, it hadn't been a great season for Alexis or Udinese, but at least it ended on a high for both. Alexis felt like he was on the verge of a massive breakthrough. Perhaps it would come at the 2010 World Cup in South Africa. His three goals had helped Chile to finish second in South American qualification, ahead of Argentina and Uruguay. Now, there were high hopes at the actual tournament. Under *Loco Bielsa*, Chile had become a formidable team, playing exciting football. Alexis was the superstar but lots of their players were at top European clubs in Spain, Italy and Germany. The team spirit was great.

Alexis had enjoyed 2007's Under-20 World Cup in Canada, but playing in a real World Cup three years later was an incredible experience. As well as thirty-two national squads from all over the world, all their fans were there with their flags, shirts – and *vuvuzelas*; everywhere they went, supporters were blowing these plastic horns as loudly as they could. It took Alexis a while to take it all in – the colour, the atmosphere and the noise. He was still only twenty-one years old.

'Can you believe we're here?' he said to Arturo as they arrived for their first World Cup game against Honduras. He had a massive smile on his face as he watched the Chile fans making their way to the stadium. They were all dressed in red and there was lots of singing and drumming. 'This is the biggest tournament in the world and we're here!'

'We're not just here to make up the numbers, though,' Arturo replied with real passion in his voice. 'We're here to win and make our country proud!'

Alexis played in all three group games as they beat Honduras and Switzerland to make it through to the next round. It was a brilliant start but unfortunately they had a very tough opponent in the Round of 16 – five times champions Brazil. The combination of

Robinho, Luis Fabiano and Kaká was just too much for *La Roja* and they lost 3–0.

Alexis was disappointed but not too upset. 'There's no shame in losing to Brazil. We're a young team and this was just the warm-up,' he told Arturo at the final whistle. 'We've learnt a lot and in four years' time, we'll be back and even better!'

CHAPTER 16

ALEXIS & ANTONIO

Alexis was determined that the 2010–11 season would be his best yet. The end of the previous season had been a success and the World Cup had given him that extra bit of desire to become one of the top players on the planet. He had learnt a lot from watching superstars like Lionel Messi, Andrés Iniesta and Thomas Müller up close – and he had one key aim for the year ahead.

'I need to score more goals,' he told Antonio in pre-season. 'We can't expect you to get them all! It's now up to me to be the second striker.'

'Don't worry, the goals will come!' Antonio replied. He loved Alexis's hunger but he didn't want him to put too much pressure on himself. That might affect his overall performance and Udinese needed his pace and creativity, too. 'Set yourself a target. Let's make it ten – that's double your total last season.'

Alexis nodded; that sounded realistic. He didn't get his first goal until the end of October against Bari, but it was worth the wait. Forty yards from goal, Alexis attacked. As he drifted towards the right, the Bari defenders didn't expect him to shoot. But *Dilla* (Squirrel), of course, had perfect balance and he hit the perfect shot into the top-left corner. Goooooooaa aaaaaaaaaaaaaaalllllllll! His teammates jumped on him and the crowd went wild.

'What a rocket!' Mauricio laughed. 'That could be a goal of the season.'

His next was a header from a cross. Alexis was really pleased to be adding new skills to his game. As they celebrated, Antonio shouted, 'We might not be tall but we can get in the right positions and we can jump!'

Sánchez and Di Natale were Serie A's new

deadliest duo. They were learning from each other; Alexis was getting better in front of goal and Antonio was getting better at creating chances for others. They were unstoppable.

'It's like you've been playing together for years,' their teammates joked. 'Are you sure you're not brothers?'

But the best was yet to come. Away at Palermo, Antonio grabbed the first goal with a clever header. A few minutes later, Alexis added a second from a goalmouth scramble. Then on the counter-attack, Antonio played Alexis through on goal. From inside his own half, he ran and ran, with defenders trailing behind. With just the goalkeeper to beat, Alexis did a brilliant double stepover to take the ball round him and score. It was a sensational goal to make it 3–0 within the first thirty minutes. When he finally caught up, Antonio jumped on him and Alexis gave his partner a piggyback. The Udinese fans cheered wildly.

They weren't done yet, though. With Alexis's help, Antonio scored a fourth and then Alexis made it five. It was Alexis's first hat-trick for Udinese and the happiest moment of his life so far. After two average seasons in Italy, he was finally showing the world what he could really do. After each goal, the teammates would lift the scorer up into the air like a trophy. In the second half, Alexis scored his fourth and Antonio got his hat-trick from the penalty spot.

'*Seven-nil, seven-nil, seven-nil!*' the whole team chanted in the changing room after the game. There was a real party atmosphere, and Alexis was at the centre of it. His hard work was paying off and the biggest clubs were watching.

Mauricio even had a great statistic for Alexis: 'You're now the most successful Chilean in Serie A history. Zamorano and Salas never scored four goals in one match!'

Alexis finished with twelve goals and twelve assists, well ahead of his target. Antonio scored twenty-eight and they were both named in the Serie A Team of the Season. Thanks to them, Udinese finished fourth and qualified for the Champions League playoffs. In the *FIFA.com* World's Most

Promising Youngster competition, Alexis beat Gareth Bale and Neymar to win the award.

'What a year!' Antonio said as they waved to the fans after the final game. 'But now I'm worried – I don't want to lose the best strike partner I've ever had!'

Alexis was happy in Italy and had a lot of love for the club that had believed in him from a very young age. However, his heart was set on playing for one of the European giants. After a great season, that suddenly looked very likely. Udinese's £32 million price-tag wasn't putting anyone off. Manchester City and Manchester United were fighting each other, but Alexis preferred a move to Spain.

'At Barcelona, I can become the best,' he told his brother, Humberto, as he waited for more news. 'With Pep Guardiola as my manager and Messi, Xavi and Iniesta as my teammates, I'll win everything. It's a really big challenge but I'm ready for it!'

Alexis was back in South America to play at the Copa América. Chile were one of the favourites to win the tournament but it was hard to concentrate

on football with all of the transfer talk. Alexis just
wanted everything sorted out, but despite a quick
flight to Spain, the discussions were still going on.
After winning their group, Chile suffered a shock
defeat to Venezuela. It was a really frustrating match
for Alexis because he couldn't find any space to
create the magic they needed.

'I'm sorry, I feel like I've let you down,' he told the
squad after the game. The dressing room was silent.

'No, you haven't!' Arturo told him, putting an arm
around him. He knew that his friend was under a lot
of stress. 'You can't win tournaments on your own.
The whole team didn't play well enough but we'll
be back!'

Finally, the deal was done and Alexis signed for
Barcelona. He would be playing for the biggest team
in the world, who had won the Champions League
three times in the last five years. With Messi playing
through the middle, he would be fighting against
Pedro and David Villa for one of the wide spots in
the front three.

'Alexis is very young but he is exactly the kind

of attacking player we need,' Pep Guardiola told the world.

Barcelona had paid a lot of money for him, the second biggest fee in their club history. Now Alexis was determined to live up to the fans' huge expectations.

'I want to learn from Messi and Xavi and I want to win more titles for the club.'

CHAPTER 17

BEGINNING AT BARÇA

Alexis knew it wouldn't be easy. He was playing in a new country for a new club, with a new manager and new teammates. The fact that the new club was Barcelona just made it more difficult. Their exciting, passing football was world-famous and Alexis knew he would have a lot to learn if he wanted to make a name for himself at the Nou Camp.

With so many home-grown players, the Barcelona team was a tough environment for a newcomer. Alexis was a Spanish speaker but his South American dialect was very different from the Catalan language. They had a good time together but his teammates found it hard to understand him. They gave him the nickname 'Cachai?', a Chilean slang word meaning 'you know?'. Even big superstars like Thierry Henry and Zlatan Ibrahimović had struggled to fit in at Barcelona.

'You'll need to be patient,' Arturo Vidal told him. He had just signed for Juventus in another big Chilean transfer. 'And you'll need to adapt, Alexis. When you get the ball, you just want to go forward but that's not the way they play. Sometimes they like to pass and pass and pass, in order to keep possession. Also, don't forget that Messi is the superstar, not you!'

'I know, I know,' Alexis replied. 'I'm here to learn but I'm also here to bring something different. Pep Guardiola says he wants a more direct option in attack, so that's what I'll be. I'll give everything I can for the team – that's all I can do.'

Barcelona was a beautiful city and everyone was football-mad. Alexis was famous now and it was hard to walk around without being spotted. Before the season started, his brother came to visit him. As Alexis showed Humberto round all the city's amazing tourist sites, it really helped him settle in at his new home.

'Humberto, would you like to come to the Nou Camp today?' Alexis asked after a couple of days but he already knew the answer. It was the main reason why his brother had travelled all the way from Chile.

'Can I meet Messi?' was his brother's instant response. Alexis smiled and nodded.

When the Ballon d'Or winner shook his hand and spoke to him, Humberto nearly fainted. He had planned lots of things to say to his hero but he was in total shock. It was pretty cool having a brother who was a top footballer.

'Thanks for embarrassing me!' Alexis said afterwards with a smile. 'He's just a normal guy.'

When Humberto went back to Chile, Alexis focused on the task ahead. He knew that he needed to start his Barcelona career well, and where better to win over the fans than in the *Supercopa* against arch-rivals Real Madrid? He was really excited to start the away leg alongside Messi and David Villa. Warming up before the game, Alexis tried to take really deep breaths and not let the noise and the size of the Bernabéu Stadium scare him. It was just another game.

It wasn't the dream debut that Alexis was hoping for but he played the whole game and helped set up a goal for Messi. It would take him some time to get used to being a real team player, rather than the star player, but this was a good start.

'Well done, Alexis,' Pep said after the game. 'You worked really hard and played for the team. That's what we're looking for.'

He was in the team again for the first game of the La Liga season against Villarreal. In the first minute of the second half, Alexis was through on goal. Teammates ran up to support him but there was no way he was passing. He set his sights on the bottom left corner and put the ball there with a perfect finish. It was his first goal for Barcelona and Alexis was so excited that he took his shirt off and flexed his muscles. This was becoming his trademark celebration. He got a yellow card but nothing could ruin his big day.

'What a start to the season!' Alexis told Humberto, who had seen the game on TV. 'I love playing for this team!'

Sadly, Alexis soon picked up a hamstring injury and he needed a stretcher to carry him off the pitch. He had been very lucky with his fitness until now and that made the injury all the harder to take.

'Sorry, you're looking at six to eight weeks out,' the Barcelona physio told him the next day. 'And that's only if you rest it properly. You can't rush these things.'

Patience wasn't one of Alexis's strengths and watching others play football wasn't one of his favourite things. It was especially tough when his teammates were winning game after game without him. He needed to get back to fitness as quickly as possible.

'Don't worry so much!' Arturo told him. 'As soon as you're healthy again, you'll be back in the team scoring lots of goals.'

Alexis found his form again just in time for the next El Clásico at the Bernabéu. Real Madrid took the lead within just twenty seconds but Barcelona didn't panic. There was so much confidence in the dressing room and Alexis was learning that winning mentality. After half an hour, Messi dribbled forward and played it through to him. There were two defenders next to him, so Alexis knew he had to shoot quickly. He did what he did best by now: he shot low and hard to make it four goals in three league games. A 3–1 victory was a great result.

'Well played today,' Barcelona captain Carles Puyol said to him afterwards. 'If you want to become a fans' favourite here, those are the games to score in!'

Next up for Alexis was his first experience of the Champions League. He approached it like every other challenge in his career – with excitement and confidence. This was what he'd been working towards, the biggest stage in European football. Away at Bayer Leverkusen in the Round of 16, Alexis scored twice to set up an easy win.

'You have a really bright future,' Pep said, putting

an arm around him. To hear that from the best manager in the world was a great feeling. 'You've got the talent and you're humble and eager to learn. That's a special combination.'

By the last few months of the season, Alexis was exhausted. He wasn't used to playing so many games in so many different competitions. Despite his injuries, he had played more games than he had at Udinese. He needed a rest and there was nothing he could do to stop Barcelona going out of the Champions League against Chelsea or losing the La Liga title to Real Madrid. Alexis played in the *Copa del Rey* triumph over Athletic Bilbao, but it was his attacking rival Pedro who stole the show with two goals.

'It's been a good first year but I can do better,' Alexis said to Arturo when they met up for international duty in June 2012. A record of fifteen goals in forty-one games wasn't bad at all but Alexis always set his targets very high, saying, 'Next season, I want to win La Liga and the Champions League.'

Arturo smiled; he hoped his friend would always remain this hungry.

CHAPTER 18

THE WONDER BOY IS BACK

Alexis had big plans for the 2012–13 new season, but first he needed to get his starting spot back. New Barcelona manager Tito Vilanova seemed to prefer Cristian Tello, a new Spanish forward from the youth team. Alexis wasn't getting goals and that worried him. He was wearing the Number 9 shirt but he wasn't playing like a top striker.

'That's not the only thing you're there for, though,' Antonio Di Natale told his old teammate when he asked for some advice. 'Messi is scoring for fun right now, so just make sure you're creating chances for him.'

Alexis kept working hard but he wasn't first choice

anymore. The previous season had been stop-start because of injury; this season was stop-start because of form. He was getting into good positions but finding the back of the net was a big problem. He was on the bench for the big game against Real Madrid and when he came on, he couldn't help to find a winner.

'I really need to get that first league goal of the season,' he admitted to captain Carles. Normally he tried to look strong in front of his teammates but sometimes it was important to share things. The fans had started booing Alexis if he lost the ball or shot wide. That really upset him.

'Yes I know, but the more you think about that, the more difficult it gets,' Carles replied. 'If you keep believing in yourself, then that goal will come and then loads more will follow!'

The last thing Alexis needed was another spell on the sidelines but, in November 2012 while playing for Chile, he damaged a ligament in his right foot. Tito was furious; he didn't like how tired Alexis was after his quick trips to South America, and now his player had picked up a serious injury. International football was really hurting Alexis's club career.

'Perhaps a month's rest will be a good thing,' Martina told Alexis on the phone, trying to sound positive. She couldn't remember the last time she had heard her son sound so low. 'You're putting so much pressure on yourself and that's not helping.'

Alexis returned to the pitch with a little more self-belief but he still didn't get his first league goal until the following February. It had been a really long wait but that goal was a big turning point in Alexis's season. He scored seven more in the final fifteen games. Suddenly the confidence was back and so were the stepovers, tricks and flicks. He was attacking defenders with pace again and creating chances for his teammates. He even scored a couple of headers.

'The Wonder Boy is back!' Gerard Piqué shouted as they celebrated yet another win.

Barcelona won La Liga with one hundred points,

fifteen more than second-placed Real Madrid. Alexis was pleased with his league winners' medal but he still wasn't satisfied with his own performance. Eleven goals and nine assists in forty-six games was solid but not spectacular, and spectacular was what Alexis needed if he wanted to play up front with Messi week in week out.

'I'm twenty-four years old and I should be close to my best by now,' he told Arturo. 'I want to be a star player, not a squad player. But I need to be more consistent if I want to be one of the best players in the world.'

Time was running out for Alexis at Barcelona. Three years earlier, he had been named the world's most promising youngster. Now, the media were calling him a flop for not finding the exciting form that they'd seen from him at Udinese. Critics said he had got lost in Messi's shadow. Rumours suggested that the club were willing to get rid of their Chilean forward and that Manchester City and Liverpool were both interested in signing him.

'Is it true that Barcelona want to sell me?' Alexis asked his agent during the summer break.

Fernando could see the worry on his face and he chose his words carefully. 'They haven't confirmed it yet but I think so. But don't worry, we've got lots of offers and you deserve better! You can't be the star here and you can't play with your natural flair.'

Alexis, however, wasn't ready to give up on his career in Spain just yet. Instead, he worked harder than ever over the summer. David Villa had been sold but Barcelona had spent over £50 million to replace him with Brazilian wonderkid, Neymar. To get picked ahead of Pedro or Neymar, Alexis would have to perform at his very best in every game. It was make-or-break time.

'This season, I can't leave it seven months to score my first league goal!' he joked to brother Humberto.

Thankfully, in the opening La Liga game of the 2013–14 season against Levante, Alexis's first league goal came after just three minutes. It was a simple tap-in but it felt so good to get started. 'That's one Antonio would be proud of!' he thought to himself as he ran back to his own half. Throughout the game he looked dangerous on the right side of the Barcelona attack. His team would win 7–0.

'I reckon we have the four best forwards in the world!' Carles shouted in the dressing room after the game.

Alexis loved the sound of that. Now that he was scoring regularly again, he focused on scoring important goals. Getting one or two goals as part of a commanding victory was good but scoring winners in high-pressure games was what true superstars did. Alexis was learning from the master himself – he had seen Messi do it time and time again.

Against Sevilla, the match was tied 2–2 with seconds to go. Messi dribbled towards goal and pulled the ball back just before the by-line. The goalkeeper deflected it out and Alexis was there to react first and smash it into the net. He had scored the winner in a really tough match. It was one of his favourite goals for Barcelona, and a sure sign that he was becoming the world-class player he wanted to be.

CHAPTER 19

THE RIGHT PLACE AT THE RIGHT TIME

'The right place at the right time!' Alexis said to his teammates. How many times had he heard Antonio say that to him at Udinese? He had a lot to thank his old strike partner for.

Three weeks after the Sevilla game, Barcelona were 1–0 down to Real Valladolid. Alexis didn't panic; he was determined to be the match winner again. Four minutes later, he got the ball on the right wing and ran at the defence. As they backed away in fear, Alexis saw he had the space to shoot. From outside the penalty area he hit the perfect shot, powerful and swerving, into the top corner. Xavi ran to celebrate with Alexis; he was an

important player for the club now and that
felt good.

'That's four league goals already and it's early
October!' Alexis told his brother happily on the
phone.

'That's twice as many as Neymar has scored!'
Humberto joked.

Alexis and his Brazilian teammate Neymar were
friendly rivals. They got on well and always tried
to help each other to score but they were also
competing to start alongside Messi. Alexis was
pleased to have more goals. He needed to keep
that going.

Against Real Madrid later that same October,
Barcelona's then-manager Tata Martino picked Neymar
to start. Alexis was very disappointed to be on the
bench for such a big game but he knew he could still
play a crucial role. After seventy minutes, Barcelona
were winning 1–0 but they wanted another goal. It was
very rare for Ronaldo, Bale and Di María not to score
at least one. They had lots of chances but so far they
hadn't found the net. Alexis came on for Cesc Fàbregas.

'Use your energy,' Tata told him. 'There's space on the counter-attack and their defence is getting tired!'

Five minutes later, Neymar played a great ball down the right. With his incredible pace, Alexis beat two Madrid defenders to the ball but he still needed to do something special to score. He saw that the goalkeeper had come off his line. As the defenders came to tackle him, Alexis kept calm and chipped the ball brilliantly over the keeper's head and into the back of the net. What a goal! He had never heard the fans cheer his name so loudly. He was the hero and he loved it. Real Madrid scored a goal in stoppage time but thanks to Alexis, Barcelona had won the game.

'Wow, that was a brilliant goal!' Messi told him at the final whistle, giving him a big hug. 'Even I probably wouldn't have tried that in such an important match!'

It was great to receive praise from such a massive superstar. If he kept working hard, Alexis was sure he could reach that level. It had taken a few years but he now felt comfortable in Spanish football, playing the Barcelona way. The media was no longer saying that Alexis should be sold. He was in the best form of his life. Three days later, Alexis made his one hundredth appearance for Barcelona in a match against Celta Vigo. It was a real honour to have played so many games for one of the biggest teams in the world.

'I'm going to celebrate with more goals!' he told his mum, full of confidence.

Within ten minutes of kick-off against Celta Vigo, Cesc had taken a shot and Alexis had scored the rebound. Another three days later, Alexis scored another matchwinner, this time against Espanyol. There was no stopping him now. He had completely won over the fans; now they clapped him every time he touched the ball.

'Do you remember when you thought you'd never score?' Carles asked Alexis with a smile, as they thanked the fans after another victory. 'Now, you score every game!'

Alexis had never felt so good. He had always worked hard but now he had a new self-belief and focus. There were rumours that he was the top transfer target for the big clubs in England – Manchester United, Arsenal, Liverpool and Manchester City. Their interest increased that same autumn when Chile played an international friendly against England in London.

'Go out and show them what they're missing!' Arturo joked in the tunnel before kick-off.

Alexis scored his first with a header into the bottom corner and then made sure of victory in the last minute with another lovely chip. He was a world-class player now. The English media said he was 'the best player on the pitch' and hoped Alexis would be bringing his talent to the Premier League soon. It was nice to be admired but as long as Barcelona wanted him, Alexis wanted to stay.

'I need a new target,' he told Arturo as they got ready to go back to their clubs.

'What about a hat-trick?' Arturo suggested. 'You scored one in Italy and now you need to score one in Spain. Messi seems to do it every week!'

Alexis liked that idea and he made it his aim for the New Year. First, however, he went home to Tocopilla for Christmas. He did it every year now and he looked forward to doing so for months. It was a great way to catch up with his friends and family and the town went wild every time their hero returned. Just as he had promised his friend Gustavo many years earlier, Alexis rode through the streets on a float, handing out signed footballs to all of the children.

'The kids look so happy!' he said to his mum, Martina. She loved her son's visits, even if she did have to share him with everyone else. 'It feels good to give something back to the town where I grew up.'

This year was extra special. Alexis had given lots of money to build new football pitches in the town and the local council had decided to rename a street after him. The *Cuarta Poniente*, where he used to play football at *Cancha Lazareto*, was now called *Alexis Sánchez*. It was such an honour to have his name on the road sign. Not only this – they had also painted a big mural on the wall. It showed Alexis playing for Chile, next to the shirts of all of the clubs he had played for – Barcelona, Udinese, River Plate, Colo Colo, Cobreloa and, most important of all, Club Arauco de Tocopilla.

'I don't know what to say,' was Alexis's emotional response. His friends and family had never seen him so lost for words. 'Thank you so much!'

The holiday gave Alexis a rest from football and it also reminded him just how many people looked up to him back home. He wanted to show every Chilean child that anything was possible if you worked hard enough.

With this inspiration inside Alexis, it only took him five days of 2014 to achieve his New-Year aim. His first goal in a home game against Elche was a striker's finish, smashing Jordi Alba's cross into the back of the net. His second was a tap-in after a nice pass from Pedro.

'This is it,' Alexis thought to himself as he ran back for the kick-off. Five minutes later, Barcelona won a free-kick thirty yards from goal. Without

Neymar or Messi, Alexis stepped up to take it and non-one argued.

With a short run-up, he curled the ball up over the wall and into the corner of the net. There was nothing that the goalkeeper could do because it was hit with so much power. Tata clapped and clapped with a big smile on his face. 'Alexis the Superstar' was the headline in the newspapers the next day. Alexis cut it out and sent it to his mum for the scrapbook.

It wasn't a great season for Barcelona, but it certainly was for Alexis. He finished with twenty-one goals, his best ever total. Only Messi, Ronaldo and Atletico Madrid's Diego Costa had scored more in La Liga and he also got ten assists. Alexis had turned everything around at the Nou Camp and now it was time to light up the World Cup in Brazil.

CHAPTER 20

HEARTBREAK IN BRAZIL

'We can do this!' Alexis told his teammates as they huddled near the halfway line. A lot of players were sitting down and the physios were trying to shake the cramp out of tired legs.

Their second-round match against the 2014 World Cup hosts Brazil was going to penalties. It had been a really tight game and in the last of the 120 minutes, Mauricio Pinilla had hit the crossbar. Chile had come so close to winning but it wasn't over yet. Arturo and Eduardo had both been substituted, so Alexis needed to be the team leader.

'I'll take one,' Alexis told the coach, Jorge

Sampaoli, straight away. He didn't have much energy left but he knew this was his responsibility.

It had been a great tournament so far for Alexis and for Chile. Thousands of their fans had travelled thousands of miles to Brazil in buses and cars decorated with the colours of the national flag – red, blue and white. The atmosphere was incredible. Chile had their best squad ever and *Loco Bielsa* had turned them into a winning team. Alexis was the star but Arturo was a great midfielder, Claudio Bravo was a great goalkeeper and Eduardo Vargas was scoring lots of goals. There were lots of other talented players too like Gary Medel and Charles Aránguiz. They played attacking football and they could beat anyone.

Alexis had scored three goals in the tournament already – one in their opening win against Australia, one in their shock victory over Spain to get revenge for their defeat at the 2010 World Cup group stages, and now one against Brazil. None of the goals had been spectacular but they were all really important, especially the equaliser against the hosts. Eduardo had won the ball and passed it to Alexis just inside the penalty area. A defender came towards him – did he have time to take a touch before shooting? Alexis decided that he did. He controlled the ball and then placed it in the bottom corner. Goooooooooooooaaaa aaaaaaaaaaaaaaaaaaallllllllllllllll!!!

'Come on!' he shouted as they all celebrated. '*Vamos Chile*!'

They couldn't quite find the winner and so penalties would decide which team went through to the quarter-finals. All of the Chile players hugged and encouraged Claudio Bravo, their experienced goalkeeper. They needed him to be the hero with some great saves.

Alexis took their second, after Júlio César had saved Mauricio Pinilla's strike. David Luiz had scored Brazil's first penalty but Willian dragged his wide. Chile had another chance to equalise.

'You can do it!' Arturo shouted, patting Alexis on the back. He had faith in his friend and teammate.

As he made the long walk from the halfway line, Alexis focused on finding that bottom left corner. Júlio César was really good at saving penalties so he would need to hit the ball hard. Alexis put the ball on the spot and looked up at the goal. He then measured his run-up and took a long, deep breath. These were the big moments where he needed to stay calm and perform well.

Alexis stepped up and kicked the ball with as much power as he could. It was heading for that bottom left corner but unfortunately, Júlio César had guessed right. He dived low and made a brilliant save. Alexis just stood there with his head in his hands. The Brazil fans were going wild behind the goal. He couldn't believe it.

Slowly, Alexis walked back to the halfway line. His teammates tried to comfort him but he was in shock. He almost always scored his penalties. Alexis found it very hard to watch the rest of the shoot-out. Marcelo made it 2–0 but then Charles pulled one back, Claudio saved from Hulk and Marcelo Díaz made it 2–2. The Chile players and supporters cheered loudly – they were back in the game.

'*Vamos Chile!*'

Neymar scored his penalty and so the pressure was

on defender Gonzalo Jara. As his shot hit the post and went wide, the Brazil players ran to celebrate with their goalkeeper.

'It's not your fault,' Arturo said, trying to make Alexis feel better. He was still sitting on the halfway line long after the match was over. He was too upset to say anything. 'We fought hard and we have to be proud of what we did.'

Alexis knew Arturo was right but he hated losing, especially when they had come so close to winning. He would never forget the pain of missing that penalty. He felt like he had let his country down. In his head he went over it again and again. Should he have hit it high? Did he make it too obvious that he would put it to the left?

'We were the better team and we should be in the quarter-final,' Alexis said to himself, wiping away the tears with his shirt.

Alexis hoped a holiday would help him to move on. Then he would think about next season and qualifying for the next World Cup in 2018.

'I'm only twenty-five,' he told Arturo, once he

was feeling a bit better, 'and you're only twenty-seven. We can both play in at least another two tournaments!'

Back in Europe, the media were saying that Barcelona would sign Uruguayan striker Luis Suárez for over £50 million. Alexis wasn't afraid to fight for his place but it was clear that the club didn't really believe in him.

'They have Neymar and Messi and they clearly don't think I'm good enough to be the third forward,' he told his brother. He'd hoped that his form during the previous season would keep him in the team.

'Don't give up yet,' Humberto said. 'It might not be true but if it is, then there are thousands of clubs that will want to sign you.'

In the end, Alexis left Barcelona on the day that Luis arrived. Lots of big European teams tried to buy him but Alexis made up his mind quickly.

'Arsenal play beautiful football,' he told Fernando, his agent. Their manager Arsène Wenger had come to speak to him at the World Cup to persuade him to move to London. 'Barcelona play beautiful football too but they care so much about keeping hold of the ball. Arsenal want to score every time they have the ball. They play like Chile and that's the style I love!'

Alexis wanted to be a first-choice star and he wanted the chance to win lots of trophies. At Arsenal, this could all come true. Mesut Özil, Santi Cazorla, Olivier Giroud, Jack Wilshere, Per Mertesacker – there were lots of top international players in the squad. Wenger was an excellent manager who could help Alexis get even better. So, in July 2014, and for £35 million, he became the Gunners' second most expensive player ever. Alexis was used to being a big-money signing, but this time he was determined to prove his talent value straight away.

CHAPTER 21

GUNNING
FOR GLORY

'Welcome to Arsenal!' Mikel Arteta said when Alexis
arrived at the training centre. 'I'm a big Barcelona
fan, so I know a lot about you already. Your pace is
going to be perfect for us.'

Alexis settled into London life very quickly.
It was a lively city with so much to see and do.
Again, Humberto flew over to help him settle in
and together the Sánchez brothers visited Big Ben,
Buckingham Palace and the Tower of London.

'There's no Messi here but I prefer London
to Barcelona!' Humberto said as they bade their
goodbyes at the airport.

Alexis couldn't speak any English, so he started

having lessons twice a week. Until he got better at the language, he would need Mikel, Santi Cazorla and Nacho Monreal to translate for him. Luckily, Arsène Wenger also spoke very good Spanish. In training, 'the Spanish Armada' were unstoppable. In a five-a-side game, David Ospina rolled the ball to Nacho, who passed to Mikel, who played it to Santi. Santi passed to Alexis who beat his defender with a brilliant bit of skill. After a neat one-two with Santi, Alexis fired past Wojciech Szczesny.

'He's in the same league as Messi and Ronaldo,' Carl Jenkinson said afterwards. Everyone was very impressed with Alexis's energy and desire.

'Most players don't really like training,' Arsène said to him, 'but you seem to love it. You don't walk out onto that field… you run!'

'I want to be the best player in the world and I want Arsenal to be the best team in the world,' Alexis replied with fire in his eyes. Those were his aims for the new season and he would work hard to achieve them.

Alexis's first match for Arsenal was the FA

Community Shield in August 2014 against
champions Manchester City. From the right side of
the attack, he played a key role in setting up goals
for Santi and Aaron Ramsey. In the last minute of the
first-half, he exchanged a one-two with Yaya Sanogo.
Alexis ran as fast as he could to reach the pass but he
couldn't quite get there before the Manchester City
goalkeeper. As he got back to his feet, the Arsenal
fans cheered Alexis for his effort. They had a new
favourite player.

Alexis was taken off at half-time. He was very tired
but he had really enjoyed his debut, saying, 'Wow,
the speed of the game here is incredible!'

Alexis immediately became the Premier League's
most exciting player to watch. He loved to beat
defenders with his flicks and tricks and he created
lots of chances for his teammates. All he needed was
a goal of his own. Just three weeks later, away at
Leicester City, a shot from Yaya Sanogo was saved
but Alexis was there to put the ball in the net. He
preferred to score great goals but they all counted
and he was so happy to get that first one. So were

the fans. They had a song for him already – '*Alexis Sánchez baby, Alexis Sánchez oooooooohhhhhhh*'.

'The Premiership is so competitive,' Alexis said to Aaron after the game had ended 1–1. 'In Spain, the top teams expect to win a lot of games quite easily but here, every game is very difficult to win. All of the teams run and fight from start to finish. I love it!'

Alexis was on the bench for his first North London derby against Tottenham Hotspur. It was disappointing but Arsène didn't want his star player to play too much football too quickly. The Arsenal manager had seen so many new players fade after the first couple of months. Alexis sat impatiently on the bench, unable to stay still. He couldn't wait to get on the pitch, especially when Tottenham took the lead. He had thirty minutes to help win the game for Arsenal. With fifteen minutes left, Alexis crossed to Santi and his shot eventually fell to Alex Oxlade-Chamberlain to score. A derby draw wasn't great but it was definitely better than a derby defeat.

'I've had a little rest,' Alexis told Mikel, 'and now I'm ready to show what I can do!'

Alexis scored in four games in a row to make it eight goals after eleven league games. It was one of the best starts the Premier League had ever seen and Arsenal legend Thierry Henry had called Alexis the club's best signing in six years. In the Champions League, he had scored three goals in five games to help the Gunners qualify for the second round.

'Everyone said it would take me a long time to adapt to English football,' Alexis said to Humberto after winning a third Arsenal Player of the Month award in a row. 'I think it took me about thirty minutes!'

Everyone was talking about the 'Alexis impact'. The newspapers said that without his goals and assists, the Gunners would be down in mid-table. He was the perfect fit, adding pace and power to a team that sometimes looked scared to shoot. Even Luis Suárez had only scored four times in his first three months.

'They're saying on *Match of the Day* that Arsenal are a one-man team!' Santi joked as Arsenal's Spanish-speaking players had dinner together. Alexis felt really comfortable at the club and loved the strong team spirit. He had a new nickname; they called him 'Duracell' because of his endless energy. He was very happy with his decision to leave Barcelona.

Even after grabbing a last-minute winner against Southampton, though, Alexis still wasn't satisfied. 'The best players change the biggest games,' he said. 'That's what I need to do now.'

CHAPTER 22

PREMIER LEAGUE LIFE

'We need to be careful with you,' Arsène told Alexis ahead of the busy Christmas schedule. 'Even the best players get tired when they first come to England. It's a tough league and there's no winter break.'

Alexis understood but he wanted to play every minute of every game. He had to cancel his yearly trip back to Chile to hand out presents because his club needed him. His form wasn't as amazing as earlier in the season but he was still scoring goals. As they chased a top-four spot, Arsenal couldn't afford to leave him out. His teammates passed the ball nicely but Alexis added something different. He dribbled around defenders and he scored goals.

'I can rest when I retire,' he liked to tell everyone. Sadly, a hamstring injury gave Alexis no choice but to rest.

'This is your little winter break,' Arsène told him at the training centre. He needed his superstar to stay positive. 'Please, please, please take it easy and let your injury heal!'

Relaxing wasn't one of Alexis's strengths. Without football, he was very grumpy. Mikel was also injured and so he tried to cheer Alexis up by taking him out for dinner. The worst thing was missing the North London derby. Without Alexis's flair, Arsenal were beaten 2–1. It was very hard to sit in the stands watching the game.

'I just wish I could have been out there,' he told Mikel. 'I should be ready for the next match, though.'

Alexis lasted seventy minutes against Leicester City but his knee was hurting. If he wasn't feeling one hundred per cent, he couldn't give his all for the team.

Arsène made him miss the next few matches,

explaining: 'Alexis, the next month is the most important month of the season. We have massive games in the Champions League, the FA Cup and the Premier League. I need you fit!'

Alexis loved playing in the Champions League but sadly he couldn't find his best form to rescue Arsenal. They were favourites to beat French side Monaco but they lost 3–1 at home. It was a real shock.

'Today our defence let us down,' Arsène said, putting an arm around Alexis at the final whistle. He knew how hard the Chilean had tried, and he still had a slight injury.

They won the away leg 2–0 but it wasn't quite enough. In the changing room afterwards, Alexis tried to keep up the team spirit, saying: 'We're out of one competition, so now we focus on winning the other two!'

He was one of the most popular players at the club; they loved his positive attitude. Alexis never stopped smiling because he knew how lucky he was to be doing what he loved. They could all learn a lot from him. Inspired by Alexis's words,

Arsenal won six Premier League matches in a row. Alexis needed time to get back to his best but with Mesut, Olivier and Santi in unstoppable form, he had that time.

With the Gunners 2–0 up against rivals Liverpool, the ball came to Alexis on the left. Kolo Touré dived in for the tackle but Alexis quickly dodged him with some lovely footwork. He was finally feeling like himself again. He had his energy back and his confidence too. At the edge of the penalty area, Alexis hit the ball straight into the top corner. The shot was so powerful that the goalkeeper hardly even saw it.

'That's the Alexis we know and love!' Olivier shouted as they celebrated with the fans.

Chelsea were too far ahead at the top of the league but with wins like that, Arsenal were making sure that they finished in the top four. That's what they needed to play Champions League football again the next year.

'Last season we were fourth, so this season we want to be third at least!' captain Per Mertesacker told them after the game. They had seven league games to go, plus a cup semi-final. Alexis still had plenty left to play for in his first season in England.

CHAPTER 23

TROPHY
TIME

'They might be a Championship team but this
is going to be a hard game,' Per told his Arsenal
teammates as they waited to head out on to the
Wembley pitch. If they took it easy, Reading would
beat them. They were only one league below and
they had some very good players.

Alexis was in high spirits. Earlier in the week,
the Professional Footballers' Association named the
shortlist for their Player of the Year Award, and he
was on it. It was likely that Chelsea's Eden Hazard
would be the winner but it was still a real honour to
make the final six.

What a first season it was turning out to be for Alexis. His Number 17 was the second bestselling shirt in the whole Premier League. Everywhere he went people recognised him and asked for selfies with him.

'It's strange; I don't feel like a famous person,' Alexis told his brother on the phone. 'I'm just a normal guy who's good at football!'

'Not just good,' Humberto joked. 'Great!'

Alexis needed a trophy to make it a perfect season. With the first half nearly over, Arsenal still hadn't scored. The supporters were getting restless. Then Mesut played a brilliant ball through to Alexis in the box. A defender came across to block him but he calmly dummied the shot and then passed it through the goalkeeper's legs.

'That was world-class!' Mesut shouted.

'No, your pass was world-class!' Alexis replied, pointing back at him to show his thanks.

Arsenal almost scored again but then suddenly, Reading were level with a really lucky goal. Arsenal had to up their game but they missed chance after chance. The game went to extra-time and the Arsenal fans cried out for their hero.

Alexis Sánchez baby, Alexis Sánchez oooohhhhhhhh!

In his trademark style, Alexis got the ball on the left, cut inside and shot for goal. It wasn't his best strike but the Reading goalkeeper was tired and he let the ball through his legs. Yet again, Alexis had scored the goal that Arsenal needed.

'Alexis saves the day again!' Santi joked afterwards. They were all relieved to be heading back to Wembley in six weeks for the final.

Back in the Premier League, Arsenal got the third place they wanted and Alexis was their top-scorer with sixteen goals. In total, he had twenty-four goals, a great record for an attacker who wasn't even a striker. And there was still one game to go. Just days before the FA Cup Final, Alexis won the PFA Fans' Player of the Season award.

'From the day I arrived at Arsenal, I've felt so much love from the fans, and not just from the Gooners!' Alexis told the media. 'England is the home of football and I'm so proud to be playing here.'

In the FA Cup Final, Arsenal faced Aston Villa. The players were expecting another difficult match but this time, they played brilliantly together. Theo Walcott got the first, Alexis got the second and then goals from Per and Olivier made it 4–0. It was a special day for Arsenal and a really nice way to end the season.

'This is just the start for us,' Alexis told Mesut that night. 'We have the talent in this squad to win every trophy under the sun!'

From a small town in Chile, The Wonder Boy had made it all the way to Wembley and he had gone home with yet another medal. Alexis was still only twenty-six, so there was plenty of time to win many more. He had travelled across the world to improve his football skills and to become a superstar. At Arsenal, he had finally found a great manager and great teammates who loved him for his special attacking style.

After adventures in Argentina, Italy and Spain, Alexis had finally found his home in England.

ALEXIS SÁNCHEZ'S HONOURS

Colo-Colo
* ★ Campeonato Nacional (Chile) (2): 2006 Clausura, 2007 Apertura
* ★ Copa Sudamericana Runner-up: 2006

River Plate
* ★ Primera División de Argentina: 2008 Clausura

Barcelona
* ★ La Liga: 2012 – 13
* ★ Copa del Rey: 2011 – 12
* ★ Supercopa de Espana (2) : 2012, 2014

★ UEFA Super Cup: 2011

★ FIFA Club World Cup: 2011

Arsenal

★ FA Cup: 2014 – 15

★ FA Community Shield (2): 2015, 2016

Chile

★ Copa América: 2015

★ FIFA U-20 World Cup: 2007 (third place)

Individual

★ PFA Fans' Player of the Year: 2014 – 15

★ Football Supporters' Federation Player of the Year: 2015

★ Facebook Football Awards Player of the Year: 2014 – 15

★ Kid's Choice Awards' Favourite UK Footballer: 2015

★ Arsenal Player of the Season: 2014 – 15

★ PFA Team of the Yea: 2014 – 15

★ Premierleague.com Team of the Season: 2014 – 15

- ★ Serie A Player of the Month: February 2011
- ★ PFA Player of the Month: October 2014